To Joe

Your Happy Life
REALIZED

How to Stop Putting Others First and Yourself Last NOW!

You inspire me!

Be happy!

EVE ROSENBERG

Love Eve

ISBN: 978-1-7328506-0-6
Library of Congress Control Number: 2018913121

Printed in the USA by Eve Rosenberg

DISCLAIMER
This book is designed to provide general educational information about the subjects discussed and not to diagnose, treat, cure, or prevent any psychological, or emotional condition. It is not intended as a substitute for any diagnosis or treatment recommended by the reader's psychiatrist, psychologist or any other medical practitioner. Use of this book does not establish any doctor-patient relationship between the reader and the author or publisher.

The author does not assume and hereby disclaims any liability to any party for any loss, damage, or disruption caused by errors or omissions, whether such errors or omissions result from accident, negligence, or any other cause. No warranties or guarantees are expressed or implied by their choice of content for this volume, and there is no guarantee that these materials are suitable for the reader's particular purpose or situation. If you suspect you have a psychological, or emotional problem, we urge you to seek help from the appropriate specialist. This book is not intended to be a substitute for the advice of a licensed physician or mental health provider.

Readers must rely on their own judgment about their circumstances and take full responsibility for all actions and decisions made because of reading this book and applying the recommended practices.

The author has made every effort to ensure the accuracy of the information within this book was correct at the time of publication. Any perceived slights of specific persons, peoples, or organizations are unintended. All names have been changed, and any reference to a specific story or instance is coincidental.

For more information, visit Eve Rosenberg at www.LessonsLearnedInLove. com, www.PeoplePleasersReformAcademy.com or www.SayNoToYesDear.com.

For my late parents, Livia and Leslie Rosenberg, Holocaust survivors whose lives and dreams were compromised and violated in unthinkable ways. I love you and live in honor of you.

For my darling, sweet, brilliant inner child, Evie, whose dreams of making others happy have remained unrealized. And who, in that pursuit, sacrificed her dreams and joy. You are my greatest love. I choose you, bless you, and dance with you every day.

ACKNOWLEDGMENTS

Many supporters have made invaluable direct and indirect contributions to this book. Thank you, thank you, to all the teachers and players in my life. I wish I could list all of you.

To my late parents, Livia and Leslie Rosenberg, you're my greatest soulmates. You gave me life and taught me my biggest lessons.

I send profound gratitude to the late Debbie Ford. You gave me my life back as I was becoming resigned that life wouldn't work out as I'd hoped. I love and miss you.

To my sister, Judy Legare, you continue to inspire me every day.

Many heartfelt thanks to Arlene Fleischman, aka Red, who is a tremendous confidence booster in my life and a very dear friend.

Thanks to my special friend, Hermine Perl, who picked my brain and helped me get clear about writing this book.

To all my extended family and friends, you're with me in my heart, and I'm grateful to have you in my life.

A million thanks to my amazing clients over the years who have struggled with People-Pleasing. Without you, I wouldn't have been inspired to share your stories anonymously so that others can heal. This book is for you and because of you.

I want to especially thank Elisa Pike for the care you gave my elderly mother so that I could continue writing and coaching. You're an angel and a big People Pleaser, too! Read this book! I wrote it for you!

Many thanks to my voice and media coach, Ruth Sherman. You brought me out of my shell and made me shine.

I have so much gratitude for my writing coach, Sam Horn, "The Intrigue Expert." You're brilliant and have brought out the writer in me. Because of you, there will be more books to come. There are no words to describe my thanks to you.

I'm so thankful for my life coach, Mindy Schrager. You're invaluable to my existence in everything I do. I'm grateful for your support.

Thank you to my publishing coach, Diana M. Needham. Your support has been amazing; without you, this book wouldn't be published.

I offer a sincere thanks to my editor, Lisbeth Tanz. Thank you for making my book the best it can be. I'm so grateful for you and your expertise.

I have a million kisses for my dogs, Tabitha, Priscilla, and Meadow, who's crossed the Rainbow Bridge. Your love is intoxicating, and you've sat by my side as long as it took to get this book finished. You inspire me with your love.

TABLE OF CONTENTS

A Note to the Reader

Fifteen years ago, I sat alone in the dark in my small apartment in Manhattan. I'd fantasize about what it would be like to enter a witness protection program and go to a new city, a small town, or even a farm. I'd change my name to Jill or Lauren and trade my long brunette hair for a short blonde bob. No one would know me, and I could start fresh. Back then, I believed something was wrong with me. I felt crazy. I was confused as to why others seemed disinterested in me, and why I felt I didn't belong. I was untethered. I had yet to learn how sensitive and fearful I was.

In later years, I learned that I was a highly sensitive person and an empath, too. I had a vulnerable constitution that was easily controlled by others, which made me perfect for the peacemaker role in my family. I was the quiet, good girl, who was likely to follow in my mother's footsteps as a People Pleaser. My job was to make sure everyone else came first and that they were happy. To pull this off, I had to abandon my needs and desires and shape-shift into what others needed me to be. I became good at it, too. I had mastered the art of being a chameleon.

It wasn't long before I had become like my mother and took on the behavior she modeled for me. The difference was that my mother had *welcome* stamped on her doormat; mine said *go away*. I became angry. The more I did for others while sacrificing myself, the further I drifted from knowing myself. It was a very lonely and fearful existence. I became detached from my own identity and codependent in all my relationships. Before long, I was projecting on everyone around me, believing they were selfish, ungrateful, and wrong. I was exhausted and neglected, and believed I'd never get what I wanted. The people in my life weren't taking care of me, and I wasn't taking care of me either. I didn't realize what I was doing, but I knew deep down that

I was compromising and violating myself at a soul level. I couldn't articulate it back then. It felt like a physical detachment as if my head wasn't attached to my body.

I wasn't conscious of having any needs and desires of my own. We can pretend that we're not who we are, but our soul knows otherwise. When we abandon ourselves, we eventually lose ourselves, along with the opportunity to know who we are. The greatest cost of the People Pleaser is a life unrealized.

How I wish I had known then what I know now! All I needed to do was think differently, believe in myself, access my strength and confidence, and stop the behavior that had me spinning in circles. What needed to change was my thinking and the negative picture I held of myself. I needed to reclaim the self I'd abandoned in my pursuit to be loved and accepted. Then, I could get busy nurturing, honoring, and forgiving myself. I could embark on the path to deeply bonding with myself. Then, if others thought unfavorably of me, it wouldn't seem like the end of the world, and I wouldn't be at the mercy of people I couldn't control. I'd give back the responsibility of making others happy and resign as the avid People Pleaser I'd become.

I would've saved years of self-abuse, anguish, and struggle if this book had existed then. I offer this book to you as an invitation to take a shortcut on the arduous path to self-love. I invite you to make yourself the priority in your life. It's the only way you'll feel alive, learn who you are, connect deeply with others, and discover your life purpose. By realizing your life purpose, you'll be able to contribute your unique wisdom and talents to a world that needs your support more than ever before and deserves the legacy you're meant to leave behind.

To realize your happy life, you must look outside of yourself to observe how your experiences show up and to see how others treat you. Your outer world is an orchestrated reflection of how you see yourself. Understanding this will support your inward look and allow you to focus on the changes you need to make for the world outside to show up favorably. The circumstances you see reflect what you believe you deserve.

If you want to become an active player in the game of your life and learn how to attract positive circumstances and relationships, you need supportive tools and practices. You have much more control than you may believe. You're just using the wrong tools.

You can choose to stay the same and let the chips fall where they may. Either way, the chips are falling. You're participating whether you think you are or not. If you're frustrated, sad, angry, and fed up with your relationships and the negative experiences in your life, then I invite you to pick up the chips and read on.

I must caution you first: Your life and relationships will change. You'll lose some people and things along the way because not every-one or everything in your life is meant to last. The relationship with yourself is ongoing, and it needs to be nurtured and nourished. The only person who can do that effectively is you. Once you turn your attention toward yourself, you'll attract healthy, joyful relationships with others, and you'll handle your challenges more effectively and proactively. More importantly, you'll trust yourself and make the best decisions for you. My dear reader, this is *Your Happy Life Realized.*

So, let's get started. We don't have as much time as we think we do.

How to Use this Book

It can be tempting to look toward the end of the book for my recommendations on how to stop People-Pleasing; however, reading the book from the beginning will reveal the very important first steps needed to begin the process. We can't change anything we're unaware of and what we don't acknowledge. The structure of this book supports the discovery of vital information necessary to help you make sense of your People-Pleasing journey and aid your process of self-forgiveness.

My personal stories and those of my clients and friends told anonymously are provided as examples of People-Pleasing behavior and the dangers of not stopping it. My intention is for you to recognize yourself in some of these circumstances, so you realize you're not alone and that you *can* create an extraordinary life filled with healthy and happy relationships.

I hope for you a life filled with joy and limitless possibilities.

Introduction

I often imagine myself going back four-plus decades and having a fifteen-minute heart-to-heart with my seventeen-year-old self.

We meet in a quaint little tea house with beautiful china cups from all over the world encased in glass. Crystal chandeliers hang from a fourteen-foot ceiling that's painted a pale blue and adorned with puffy, white scattered clouds. The myriad crystals in the chandeliers are dazzling and form speckled designs on the surrounding walls and rustic wood floors. Several tables with distinctively colored and grained marble tabletops are scattered around the room. We sit across from each other at a small, round table. No one else is there, not even a server.

I settle into my cozy chair designed in florals of pink and gold and feel myself sink into the soft cushion and pillows. I lean forward and pour her favorite tea, an English breakfast black, into a waiting teacup. I add a spoonful of sugar and a bit of milk. As I hand her the cup, she looks at me, eager for advice. I gaze into her big, brown eyes, and then say it straight up:

"Stop hiding. Start shining. Take what you know you're good at and run with it. Sprinkle fairy dust wherever you go, and wish everyone well in your heart, especially the people who turn out to be wrong about you. They're the ones who need you to be you the most for they're not at peace."

I top off her cup to warm her tea. I assure her she doesn't need to be concerned about what others think of her. "Think well of yourself, and they'll agree. People will see you as you do. It took me a long time to learn this lesson, and it's one of the most important I've learned so far.

"It's what you believe most deeply about yourself, not who you present to the world that's important. Don't confuse the two. You'll know how others see you by what they reflect. The truth will lie in that reflection. Use this information to give yourself more love and attention, not less. You'll learn to trust yourself, and then you'll know the better choices you must make. If you find the courage to be who you are, despite what others say or do, you'll live a life that is grand and great."

I speak with conviction. "If you find yourself trying to be something you're not, you'll live a life that's tragic for you and everyone involved. You won't know your soul, and your gifts will die with you."

I reach over and put my hand on top of hers gently but firmly. "Even if you choose the latter, you must find it within your heart to forgive yourself, to get back up, and do better the next time. *You* are your greatest source. You have all the answers you need inside of you, and you have more control than you could imagine. Always look for a lesson. Learn it, and heed it, too. Lessons become opportunities when you put them to good use."

We finish our tea in silence. She looks thoughtful as if she's mulling my words in her head. Our time is almost up. I need to make sure she hears me, so I look at her inquisitively. She looks at me and nods that she has. I stand and blow her a kiss. Then I turn toward the door and never look back.

By the time this book is published, I'll have reached the milestone of sixty years old. It has been an arduous journey getting here. It's been a challenge getting to know me, which remains an ongoing process. Either way, I'm here today happy, healthy, and creating new dreams. I've learned to accept that the ones I'd envisioned as a seventeen-year-old girl won't be realized. While I can look back and acknowledge how nice it would have been to have fulfilled my young dreams, I recognize that I live an extraordinary life today even without them. I'm proof that even when things get screwed up, there's still hope for an amazing life. It may look completely different than what we predicted in our early adulthood, but it's not a bit less extraordinary. Deciding to live an extraordinary life—or not—is up to us.

I share my story so that you can see the alternate route available to you if you desire to ease your struggle in life and love. My hope for you is that you live to know yourself deeply, accept who you are despite what others think, and find the people who will celebrate and cheer you on, not because you need them too, but because you'll inspire them just by being who you are. Finally, I hope that you dance with them in ways that make your heart sing. This reality can only happen when you see your worth within your own heart and not a moment sooner.

There is no greater tragedy than living a life not knowing who you are, living a lie, or feeling obligated to live the ways others want you to live. It won't feel right. It won't bring you deep joy, and everyone will lose.

It's time to choose *you*. No one is coming on a rescue boat, and you must fight for the life you deserve. All it takes is a willingness, a good imagination, and the ability to forgive. This book will shed light on why you haven't been able to do this effectively and will support you to start doing things differently.

The life you've lived up to this point has been guiding and urging you to wake up and pay attention. Right now, you may be sad, angry, or frustrated enough to make the changes that are waiting for your direction and dare to reach out for support. Once you start down this new path, people and experiences will show up in ways that will make you celebrate. It's my hope for you and for the world that you take that first step.

I can honestly say that if I hadn't taken my first step, I wouldn't have written this book or created two websites to support you on your journey to reform from People-Pleasing.

For women: http://www.PeoplePleasersReformAcademy.com

For men: www.SayNoToYesDear.com

PART 1

THE COMMON DENOMINATOR AND THE COMMON BEHAVIOR

CHAPTER 1

TAKING OFF THE BLINDERS

*Thought can organize the world so well that you
are no longer able to see it.*

~ Anthony De Mello

At age fifty, I said those two words for the third time around: "I do."

I glowed on that day, fully believing this marriage would not only stick but would be the one I'd call extraordinary.

It was a hot Friday in August when Matt and I exchanged our vows. I was dressed in ivory lace that showed off my slender figure and long brunette hair. Matt looked dapper in his gray morning suit. The Rabbi, his wife, and the videographer were our witnesses and only guests.

I was happy. I was hopeful. I was in love.

Those feelings didn't last long.

I felt the cold marble beneath my feet as I entered the kitchen. Matt was wearing his charcoal trousers and the light blue cashmere sweater I had bought for him the year before. I loved how the color brought out the green in his eyes. His blond hair was thinning, which contradicted his young-looking physique. He appeared much younger than his early sixties. His gray suede shoes sat on the floor next to his chair. I was praying my dogs wouldn't go for them as they followed me. A Yorkie and a Brussels griffon are small, but they can do some pretty good damage when they get ahold of a shoe. Since Matt was a neat freak and took extra care of his possessions, I was on doggy patrol.

Matt was reading the paper at our high-top butcher-block table for two which was a wedding gift from my mother. The paper was covering his face, and he didn't acknowledge my presence. Because our kitchen was very small, it wasn't possible for anyone to go unnoticed, so I chalked it up to him being engrossed in a story.

After a few minutes of starting the coffee and giving the dogs their breakfast, I began to feel insulted. Matt had always been attentive to me when we shared our weekends at my apartment in the city. Now he seemed disinterested. It had been three weeks since we married and moved in together in New Jersey. At his insistence, we unpacked and organized, which left no time for us to connect. I was a little put off that he hadn't shown me around my newly adopted state—one I knew nothing about—or connected with me to celebrate our new commitment.

Suddenly, a scene flashed in my mind.

It was ten years earlier, and I was sitting in a crowded diner on the Upper East Side of Manhattan. While waiting for my food, I watched a young couple who were each reading a section of the newspaper. They couldn't see each other; the newspapers blocked the view. When their food arrived, they folded their news neatly by their plates and continued reading while they ate. They never once spoke a word to each other. When the check arrived, he paid while she read. They left together in silence. I watched as they walked up the street, still not talking or touching.

I made a judgment about that couple even though I had no other glimpse into their lives, and I promised myself that I wouldn't have a relationship like that.

This memory sparked my concern.

"Good morning," I said, breaking the silence. Matt looked up and smiled. He shared some of the news with me, and I eagerly listened.

As he got up to leave, I said with a smile, "Matt, let's set up some time in our schedules to get together and connect."

He not only resisted, but he also appeared hostile. "I have to go to work," he said brusquely. He looked as if he'd sucked on a lemon.

"Yes, me too. That's why I want to schedule in some time to see each other," I responded.

"What do you want from me?" he said, sounding annoyed.

"Seriously? Why are you putting me off? We just got married. I want to spend time with you. Is that wrong?" I wondered why he was in such a bad mood. He wasn't the Matt I knew.

"What do you think other couples do?" he asked.

"Who cares?" Now I was becoming annoyed and having a hard time understanding what was happening.

Without answering, Matt turned abruptly and walked down the hall. As he moved away, he said the five words that changed my life forever: "You're a waste of time!"

My heart took a nosedive into my solar plexus, and the pit of my stomach became numb and painful at the same time.

I stood alone in the kitchen. My mind screamed, "Did he say, 'You're a waste of time?'"

I knew what I'd heard loud and clear. I couldn't move.

Matt left without saying another word, and I hopped on a bus to Manhattan. I walked around for hours like a zombie; I almost got hit by two cabbies. I'm sure the look on my face resembled someone who had been told they had a fatal disease with less than a month to live.

If this happened now, I would pack up my things, get the marriage annulled, and move back to the city I love. But back then, if I had left, I would have missed the rest of the journey that birthed the epiphany which shocked me to my core.

Seven days after doomsday, I got the shingles virus. It made sense. A part of me began a slow death. Soon a new self would emerge: stronger, wiser, courageous, and powerful. An ordinary morning filled with an offensive exchange woke me up to the shocking realization that I believed I was, in fact, a waste of time. And Matt? He was the prince that woke me up.

I could have used this book when I think about my early experience with Matt; it would have saved me from years of struggle. On a deeper level, I believe the anguish I faced was part of my journey, and that my experience led me to write this book for myself and you. I'm grateful for everything I've endured. I hope that by reading this book, you'll be positively impacted and inspired to create an extraordinary life for yourself. By using your past circumstances as the motivating catalyst, I hope that you'll see how worthy you are and understand that any change you need to make is all up to you.

For many years, I believed people were crazy, mean, selfish, narcissistic, and offensive. I didn't recognize that I was being shown the harsh and negative picture I held of myself, which attracted the experiences I unconsciously believed I deserved. Had I known that my low self-worth and feelings of insignificance were the culprits, I could've climbed out of the deep hole I'd dug for myself long ago. Instead, I clung to my victim story feeling helpless and hopeless and creating more of the same negative experiences I was trying to escape.

Once I was willing to see myself as the *common denominator*, I was able to see the *common behavior*. I was a People Pleaser. I was sacrificing my own needs and desires for that of another, so I would be loved and accepted. I made everyone else my priority while abandoning myself and becoming dependent on others to make me happy, too. Had I been confident and strong, Matt's offensive comment wouldn't have had the impact that it did even though it was mean and inappropriate.

This experience woke me up to see the depths of my self-loathing. It was hard to swallow, but it was essential I become aware and acknowledge it to heal myself.

The experience with Matt delivered the light bulb moment that prompted all my old assumptions to begin unraveling and, eventually, led to the *mother of epiphanies* and to writing this book. From that moment on, everything in my life changed. I felt as if I'd awakened from a long trance. I had newfound confidence, and I began setting boundaries for myself and with others. I began attracting great people and extraordinary experiences. I went from losing faith to feeling alive and hopeful. I began creating new dreams, realizing I could have whatever I desired with the right mind-set and trustworthy tools.

Supporting others as an emotional wellness coach for over a decade has helped me see into my clients' lives, too, and given me the ability to recognize that their challenges consisted of hardships and heartache, much like the ones I'd experienced myself. I could also see similarities with friends and family members. When I analyzed our lives, the circumstances may have varied, but the people we were attracting were similar and the behavior we were all using publicly was the same. We were all People Pleasers. We continued the behavior patterns we had learned very early in life: doing for everyone else while leaving ourselves out; being overly concerned with what others thought about us; avoiding confrontations so as not to hurt people's feelings; and lacking the boundaries needed to gain the respect, admiration, and appreciation we craved.

We were too nice to others while compromising and violating ourselves. We negated our own needs and desires, and as a result, we lost the connection with ourselves in the pursuit to please everyone else. When we fail at this agenda, our People-Pleasing way becomes a constant tropical storm sweeping through our lives, creating toxic relationships, fostering detachment from ourselves, and sucking out any joy. Further, we begin to develop physical and emotional ailments and begin to believe that life has become an exhausting, futile burden.

CHAPTER 2

REVEALING YOUR SELF-IMAGE

*What is necessary to change a person is to change
his awareness of himself.*

~ Abraham Maslow

If I was falling off a cliff and had one sentence to shout out to the world before I crashed and died it would be, "Look to how others treat you, and you'll know how you feel about yourself."

If your life is showing up in dissatisfying and disappointing ways, it has more to do with your relationship with you. You may be hiding from yourself even more than you're hiding from others, and you may not even realize that you're hiding at all, especially if you're a People Pleaser. If you care what other people think of you, it's because deep down you believe you're not okay. If that's your truth, your circumstances will rise to meet you eagerly and prove you right. We've all met that self-fulfilling prophecy at one time or another.

Watch how others treat you for it will reveal the self-image you carry of yourself. If you're rolling your eyes, are skeptical, confused, or find this hard to believe, watch the reflection of others' behavior toward you and then consider how you exhibit that same behavior toward yourself. You'll be blown away with how accurate this exercise can be. For example, if you find that people don't support you, look at how you don't support yourself. If your spouse or children don't listen to you, look for ways that you don't listen to yourself. If the people in your life don't see you as a priority, see how you don't prioritize yourself. Your lists will become long and revealing.

You may have some resistance to doing this exercise, so let me explain why you should be jumping up and down with excitement.

You're the only person in the world you have control over. You don't have control over other people's actions, reactions, thoughts, or behaviors. So, if you change *your* behavior toward yourself, others will follow in *their* behavior toward you.

This behavior goes both ways. As people reflect their behavior toward you based on how you treat you, you'll treat them based on how they behave toward themselves. That's why relationships can be so confusing. When we get into a relationship dance, we're compelled to behave and react in ways we don't fully understand because we're taking cues from the other person's self-image.

We always attract the experiences we believe we deserve. When we're in a relationship where each party has a poor self-image, there's a status quo to the dynamic. But as we begin to improve our self-image, we may find others seem threatened by our growth. Their reaction is more likely due to their lack of awareness, unwillingness, or inability to change the way they see themselves than how they feel about us directly. They're unable to relate to us in the same way because we feel uncomfortable and unfamiliar to them. We've changed the status quo. When this happens, the relationship may decline quickly.

If we go back to my story with Matt that I shared in chapter one, his offensive treatment of me was based on my offensive treatment of me. If I had been my priority and believed I was important and worthy of other people's time and attention, I wouldn't have attracted Matt.

I invite you to embark on a journey to find out the truth you hold about yourself so that you begin to attract the experiences that bring you joy and to create healthy, intimate relationships with yourself and others. It will require your commitment to allow yourself to see things differently. You must trust in the unseen and the unknown and give up your attachment to things working out in whatever scenarios you've conjured up in your mind. Your success will depend on your willingness to change some big things in your life, starting with seeing yourself in a different light. You'll need to be tolerant and patient as you expose yourself as *the common denominator* participating in the *common behavior*: People-Pleasing. Once you see how this behavior has been wreaking havoc in your life, you'll understand that the only way to the life you want is *to stop*!

"Never praise your children!"

My mother repeated this phrase throughout my childhood. Can you imagine the effects of that?

Sitting at our dinner table, I heard stories about other people's children.

"Todd is so smart; Sarah is such a pretty little girl; the Steinberg's children will probably go to the best private school." She went on and on.

What's wrong with us? I thought. When I was old enough and had the guts to ask, she said it again.

"You must never praise your children."

I admit, as much as I've struggled, I feel bad for the generations that came before me. We have so many choices today that they didn't. If I felt "less than" about myself, I could only imagine what went on in my parents' minds about themselves. I know it wasn't good.

From the time I was a little girl, I loved to run and twirl, laugh and play, and, most of all, see people smile. I was a happy child and full of wonder. I wanted to live in a happy, safe world, and I wanted to love my family and feel their love.

Somewhere very early on, I got the impression that if I made my parents happy, we would be okay. And as impressionable as children are, I also understood we were in trouble. I couldn't identify it, but I felt it. My twin sister knew it, too, because she would act out a lot and throw tantrums.

My father used to play mind games with my mother, my sister, and me. He could be quite a bully at times. He would say things and then later say he never said them. After a while, I didn't know what to believe, although I could swear what I remembered was right. The longer it went on, the more confused I became. I began to think I was crazy.

It was the early seventies, and the psychedelic orange, yellow, and brown wallpaper in our kitchen celebrated the times. My mother, sister, and I were sitting around the kitchen table discussing some girly topics when my father walked into the room.

He was a powerful man, and I could always feel a shift in the energy each time he showed up. Reflexively, all three of us became guarded and anxious because we never knew what to expect. Many times, even his silence was enough to let us know *something* was on the horizon.

I'd often wonder what he was thinking. Most of the time, I was dead wrong. He'd verbally degrade my mother in a condescending tone, usually over her weight, calling her fat or laughing at the things she said. He didn't miss an opportunity to find ways to belittle my sister and me, too. He'd ask us questions about current events or history. He was incredibly intelligent, and I still believe deep down he was trying to teach us things.

"Did you hear what's going on in Israel now?"

I didn't have a clue. The question made me squirm in my chair. I avoided my father's gaze. The shame was overwhelming. Sometimes, I would answer his questions correctly, and I'd beam with pride. But it wasn't long before he asked a hard question that I didn't know the answer to or that I answered wrong. That's when the grin on his face would widen with pleasure. He had a sarcastic chuckle that would make me sink in my chair. To this day, I believe these incidents affected my ability to learn. I still avoid things that seem complicated or take too much effort to understand.

As I got older, I could acknowledge the verbal, mental, and emotional abuse I'd endured. I was traumatized regularly by being overly criticized or by being ignored. My mother's lack of confidence prevented her from protecting herself—much less us girls—and believed that staying in her marriage was the best option for us. I don't know if she denied the abuse inflicted on us, or if she was too traumatized to believe she could move on. Today, I'm sad that she didn't feel good enough about herself to make changes.

My parents were great people, but they were also very wounded. They had been placed in work camps during the Holocaust. After the war ended, they met in Austria and emigrated to the United States shortly after that. They couldn't speak English and struggled to find work. Therapy wasn't something they thought about. They believed people should handle their problems responsibly on their own.

Despite my parents' behavior and mind-set, I remember believing early on that I was the cat's meow, something really special, despite those early incidents. I can recall a time where I felt confident. I think most children feel this way until something happens, and then they don't. Before long, the mixed messages I was getting at home were causing me to question who I was. I became withdrawn and shy. At some point, I detached from myself.

Luckily, my sister and I were physically attractive. We were tall, thin, clear-skinned, with long, straight brunette hair and soft features. Because we were twins, we received extra attention from outsiders. I relished people noticing me, and I was popular in school. I consider this time in my life to be my saving grace. It seemed natural to continue People-Pleasing to keep myself connected to others in a positive way. Mostly, it was because I wasn't nurtured at home.

As time went on, my lack of a bond with myself became problematic. It wasn't something I was consciously aware of; I just felt that I didn't belong even as I desperately tried to fit in. My self-esteem was very low. Dr. Phil McGraw once said, "It takes one thousand *atta boys* to erase one *you're an idiot*." The scale wasn't tipped in my favor. I doubted myself and became fearful in my relationships. I relied heavily on what others needed and wanted of me.

People-Pleasing behavior begins very early in life. Think back to your childhood and ask yourself the following questions:

- What do you remember about your early experiences that gave you the impression that you were less than, unimportant, not good enough, or that you were bad, wrong, or didn't fit in?
- Did you find yourself being a *good girl* or *good boy* to please your parents?
- Did you remain quiet and stay out of the way?
- Did you have so many chores imposed on you that you felt things were unfair?
- Did you feel responsible for your siblings?
- Did you parents give you choices about what you wanted?

In your answers, you may find one or two experiences where you felt unimportant, insecure, left out, or wrong in some way. As you reflect, you may discover that at some point you made the decision to do what others needed and wanted as a way to survive your reality.

I encourage you to release any negative judgment about what you find. If you approach this exercise with curiosity and fascination, you'll learn more about yourself and how you became a People Pleaser. You'll also be on your way to transforming your relationship with yourself. The first step required for change is awareness. It's time to walk powerfully on level ground and begin to attract the experiences that will bring you joy. Our early beliefs become the themes of our lives. Realizing them will support us in using them to serve us.

"Call Dr. Fleischer! There's another baby in here!"

The nurse ran out of the room, and in two seconds flat, it sounded off the loudspeaker. "Dr. Fleischer, report to Maternity O.R. three!"

I can only speculate as to whether or not I heard it. I was there, but the sound would have been muffled for me.

My twin sister was being examined and cleaned up. Aside from being born breach, exiting the birth canal feet first, she was a healthy, beautiful girl.

I, on the other hand, was overlooked. Nestled in my mother's womb, I was left behind in the dark.

"The doctor is on the way," the nurse assured my mother. For her part, my mother was exhausted, surprised, and confused. It was the fall of 1958 and technology was limited. That my mother was carrying twins wasn't discussed in any of her doctor's visits.

Dreaming of a son, my mother picked three names: Robert, Daniel, and David. With a new baby girl, maybe two, those names wouldn't do. A few minutes later I was born, entering the world feetfirst like my sister. I let out a strong cry: another healthy, beautiful girl. Welcome, Judy and Eve.

Many spiritual mystics and mediums believe that our birth has much to do with the challenges we'll face in our lives during our journey on this planet. They believe our birth experience sets the tone for our reality in the world. If I use my dramatic entrance as a reference point for what was to come, I would say they were spot on!

Being overlooked and left behind is a challenge I have faced many times in my life. Before I did any healing work, I constantly struggled with feelings of loneliness, depression, and despair. And as the years passed, I had more and more experiences that emphasized my feeling of dread and the sense I didn't belong. As bad things continued to happen, I came to believe that this was my lot in life, that I was dealt an unfair hand, and life was always going to be difficult. It was no surprise that I continued attracting these same experiences to prove myself right. Eventually, these experiences contributed to a general anxiety disorder and even panic attacks in my early forties.

Sometimes I wonder if I was hiding at birth. I'm highly sensitive to sights and sounds and emotionally feel things more intensely than the average person. I have a strong need to get away and retreat from people and noise after one or two hours. Looking back, I see that living in New York City for twenty-seven years was detrimental to my constitution. Back then, I lived the *should* life, as in I *should* do this; I *should* live here; I *should* be that.

If my entry into the world wasn't profound enough, I was later told by my grandmother, who lived with us, that the nurse hired to care for Judy and me our first few weeks of life was drugging our formula. My grandmother witnessed her pouring liquid from a small vile into our bottles so we would sleep. She was dismissed in the middle of the night.

Soon after the nurse left, we cried like banshees incessantly through the following days and nights as we detoxed. I'm certain this early experience may have contributed to my addictive personality; it's an arguable point.

The incidents early in our lives are more telling than we may believe. Even before we can make sense of what we see and hear, we're affected by what's around us. Having information on birth and infancy is valuable because when things make sense it brings us comfort. Some circumstances may seem more significant than others. By exploring and examining our life's early events, we'll find strong connections to our present reality. Many psychologists believe our personality is fully formed by the tender age of five. Consider your answers to the following questions:

- Do you have any information surrounding your birth?
- Are there times when a familiar discomfort arises (e.g., feelings of not belonging, believing you're being left out, feeling that you're not good enough, feeling that you're different) that stops you in your tracks?
- Are you experiencing the same kinds of relationships with the same familiar challenges repeatedly?

My friend, Lucy, was told she'd almost died at birth because the umbilical cord was wrapped around her neck during delivery. She shared with me that she feels a constant sensation of pressure around her neck and that her experiences can feel strangulating at times. Sometimes she hyperventilates.

My client, Joanne, once shared that her mother went into cardiac arrest during delivery. There was a lot of chaos and urgency in the delivery room. After Joanne was born, she was taken away so that her mother could rest. Joanne revealed that there has been much drama in her life and that it's hard for her to connect with others. She believes that her birth trauma and the lack of the crucial bond she needed with her mother caused some detachment for her and affected her ability to create bonded relationships with others.

Then there's Gary, a former colleague, who told me that when he was born he was pulled out by forceps. He attributes this early experience to a lifetime of headaches and feeling intruded upon by others.

I invite you to undertake the exploration of your life, beginning at birth to now, so you can begin to make sense of how you've lived and also to create a clear picture of how you see yourself. If your mother is alive, ask her about your birth. Clarity brings comfort, and it allows for the potential of great healing and growth. Plus, it's fun to put the puzzle together.

When I was a little girl, I used to flip through my coloring books to get to the pages that had a series of dots with corresponding numbers. You couldn't tell what image would emerge until you connected the dots. Maybe it was a pony, a dog, a flower, or something else. The point is, the dots made sense *later*.

Connecting the dots from our early experiences will help us to gain clarity and understanding about the important decisions we made and learn what drives the choices we make today.

Below is another personal example of an early experience that created some powerful, negative beliefs that have affected every facet of my life.

"No!" I yelled. "We're going, and that's that!"

I pushed aside the money my grandmother offered me not to go to Joan's house. Her stocky figure was covered by a loose gray housedress that matched her silver hair. At seventy-two, she looked ten years older. Her shock at my reaction was visible. I had never spoken back to her before. At age eleven, I was surprised at my reaction, too.

Just moments before, Judy, my friend, Carol, and I had been dropped off near our homes by the orange school bus. As we turned the corner, I could see my house: a small ranch painted a reddish-brown with teal planters displaying small, yellow and white flowers on either side. We lived on a quiet street in a small suburban neighborhood in Westchester County, New York, where the people were friendly, and children played hopscotch and rode their bikes.

My grandmother was all smiles when we arrived home, although she was surprised that Carol was with us. She held the door open and directed us toward the kitchen. We sat at the table and ate some of her freshly baked chocolate chip cookies with a glass of milk. She loved to cook and bake and enjoyed watching us eat.

She was a sweet, doting woman and a big reason for the happiness I felt as a young child. Her treats were a reminder of how much I was loved and cared for. I felt closer to my grandma than to my mother. She gave the greatest hugs, and I considered her my closest confidant and found great comfort knowing she was always there.

On this day though, she seemed worried. When we told her we were going to my friend Joan's house down the street, she became almost panicky and begged us not to go. For some reason, she didn't like Joan and offered money to my sister and me not to go. I was embarrassed in front of Carol, so I pushed the money away. When my grandmother became insistent that we stay home, I shouted at her, demanding she stop. When she didn't, I directed my sister and Carol to the door.

We visited with Joan for under two hours and then headed home. Only now the street seemed eerily different. People were gathered outside their houses. It made sense once I saw the blinking red lights in my driveway. My mother's blue Ford was parked in front of an ambulance.

I spent the next hour crying and writing a letter of apology to my grandmother, hoping that she'd regain consciousness and read it. But before my mother left for the hospital, the phone rang. I listened to her conversation on the kitchen extension.

"I'm sorry. We did all we could. She had a massive stroke and passed away."

All I thought about was yelling at my grandmother that day and how my letter would never reach her. Devastated hardly explains the loss I felt and the guilt I carried for decades. I became fearful of using my voice because I was concerned that I would disappoint people so much they would die. I stuffed my anger for years and wasn't able to confront anyone or set boundaries in relationships.

This early experience created some negative beliefs around the safeness of speaking up to express how I felt. It didn't prevent me from being angry; it just stopped me from acting on it. And because I didn't feel free to share with others when I was angry with them, I became even angrier as a result. I truly believed:

- It's not safe to use my voice.
- Anger is bad and wrong.
- People die when I use my voice and express myself.

Because it felt unsafe to speak up, to use my voice and express myself, I became influenced by what everyone else around me thought. I became very agreeable and acquiesced to others to avoid confrontations. It took a lot of energy to mask my anger. People-Pleasing behavior made sense as it covered my darker side and hid me away from others and myself. Instead of speaking up, I developed migraine headaches.

Think back to your early childhood. Identify an event or situation that changed your perception of yourself, others, or the world and led you to conclude that you must *not* express your wants, needs, or desires out of fear of what doing so could do.

- What happened afterward? How did you feel? What did you make it mean about you?

- How has this belief influenced your life? What specific situations have occurred repeatedly?

When things happen to us that bring about deep feelings of negativity and unworthiness, we look for strategies and behaviors that will help us survive.

For years, these thoughts plagued me: "If I only did what my grandmother asked of me and didn't go to Joan's house. Grandma might still be alive. At least her death wouldn't be my fault."

Intellectually, I know that my actions may have contributed to my grandmother's anxiety. I also know that her death had nothing to do with my decision to say no or to express my annoyance with her that day. I'm not that powerful. What I do know is that the thoughts, beliefs, and feelings I carried around about this early incident had the power to direct my life in an unhealthy way.

My client, Barbara, remembered an event that happened when she was about five years old. She was playing outside throwing a ball back and forth with her sister Susan. Barbara would catch the ball, but it would slip out of her hands. Her sister, who was five years older, would taunt Barbara when she made mistakes.

"Slippery hands!" Susan would say each time the ball slipped through Barbara's small hands. "You can't hold on to anything!" Susan would tease. Seems like an innocent enough experience, but Barbara took these words literally, as an underdeveloped five-year-old would, and made them mean something always true about her. When Barbara recalled this incident during one of our coaching sessions, she had an epiphany that helped her understand why she struggled with relationship commitments and keeping jobs. "I don't hold on to things," she said. "That's me! Slippery hands!"

Once she realized the connection, Barbara understood that she could laugh at this belief and its hold on her. I encouraged her to summon her slippery hands and let this one go. We both laughed.

All it takes is one incident, one insult, one offense, one harsh criticism when we're young and impressionable for us to create a bad self-image.

My client, Jack, used to ride down his stair banister when he was eleven. Before long, he noticed a pleasurable feeling in his groin area as he slid down. Innocently, he shared this with his mother and grandmother and urged them to try it themselves, because it felt really good. Horrified, they scolded Jack and told him not to talk this way and forbade him to play in this way again. Jack was confused and retreated to his room, staying there for hours.

In one of our sessions, Jack recalled this story during a visualization exercise. He connected it to his struggle with what he called his "perverted tendencies" in life, and how his marriage suffered because of his infidelity and insensitive sexual requests. Jack had a hidden belief that he was bad and perverted. Because of his mother's reaction to his innocent comment about the physical feelings he experienced while sliding down the banister, Jack developed significant shame around any pleasurable sexual experience. He acted out of resentment and confusion and could now pinpoint it to how he was treated as a child. This revelation allowed him to make different choices; he even reconciled with his wife.

Think about the beliefs you created early in your life. Write down your feelings and describe the experiences that keep repeating in your life. These experiences will expose a pattern that's indicative of a theme created by a belief or group of beliefs you tell yourself about you and your life. These beliefs have been manifesting your reality.

Remember that awareness is the first step. Also recognize how powerful you are today and that you can change your beliefs. Once you make sense of how negative beliefs are affecting your life, you'll be better equipped to change your thinking. You'll be able to think positive thoughts about yourself. It might not be easy at first, but once you can think those thoughts compulsively, they'll become deeply ingrained in your psyche, just like the negative thoughts used to be.

Because we automatically seek resolutions to our childhood experiences and relationships with our family of origin, early beliefs are important to uncover. We're drawn to the familiar and recreate our past situations, leaving us feeling incomplete. We can't achieve closure. It's not a conscious process and is why many people are frustrated by their ability to attract the same negative relationships and circumstances over and over. Life is supposed to support your growth, not to keep you stuck in patterns. But patterns will continue to run the show until your awareness and understanding of what's happening, why it's happening, and what you can do about it emerges.

If you're willing to approach your past with curiosity, eagerness, and a desire to learn about why you do what you do, and your role in the experiences you attract, you'll be taking the first big step toward forgiving the past so that you can, instead, powerfully attract your dreams.

CHAPTER 3

FOR APPEARANCE'S SAKE:
THE PEOPLE PLEASER ROLE MODEL

*The most powerful role model in a child's life
is the same-sex parent.*

~ Dr. Phil McGraw

A black cloud frequently loomed over my house when I was growing up. It magically appeared when my father was in one of his gloomy moods. We knew to stay out of his way. Even at his saddest, my father's big blue eyes sparkled in the light. I thought he was God.

Eventually, his blues passed, and he was nice again. Most of the time, he'd act as if nothing happened. It was confusing. I never knew how to feel and who to be, so I mostly stayed quiet and out of the way. I even became invisible when I had to. I made it into a game I played with myself. If I needed to disappear, I would. If I needed to reappear, I did. It was magic.

"What's wrong with Daddy?" I'd ask my mother, over and over again. Sometimes I'd approach him myself and try to make him laugh, but it rarely worked, and it scared me, too.

I did something wrong, I thought. *Maybe my mother or sister upset him.* Whatever I suspected, I made it my business to do whatever

I could to make sure we all got along. Add to my list of roles: daughter, sister, peacemaker.

If my mother needed peace and quiet, I entertained my sister. If my father was angry with my mother, I comforted my mother. If my sister was throwing a temper tantrum, I assured my parents she'd be okay.

At as young as seven years old, I knew something wasn't right with my parents. I couldn't understand why we couldn't be happy or why they couldn't get along.

One day, I watched anxiously as my father chased my mother around our rectangular dining room table with its six large chairs pushed underneath. The table took up most of the room, which made it hard to maneuver around when they hosted dinner parties. It was so tight that guests had to stand if someone needed to use the bathroom.

My mother was running after my father, often bumping into the edges and shifting the chairs. Because she was squeezed into her girdle to hide the weight she was ashamed of, she was struggling to catch her breath between sobs.

My father was laughing as he clenched her chocolate bars tightly in his hands. Those chocolate bars represented a rare pleasure in her life. Her sugar addiction helped her to cope with her reality. It also contributed to her being substantially overweight.

In contrast, my father was athletic. An avid tennis player and golfer, he was much stronger than his slight build indicated. He continued laughing as he circled the table, tormenting my mother emotionally.

Eventually, they both tired and my father surrendered the bars to my mother.

"Crybaby!" he'd say with a mocking tone. "Go and eat your chocolate. Become fatter!"

My mother retreated to her room like a dog with its tail between its legs. She remained there for a couple of hours, crying and eating the chocolate I assumed. In time, she reappeared wearing a different dress with her face freshly washed and her lips donning a bright lipstick to match what she was wearing. If I hadn't witnessed what came before, I never would have suspected that anything was wrong.

My sister and I were playing quietly with our dolls. My mother summoned us to get in the car to go to the supermarket. When we returned, she spent the rest of the day cooking beef stroganoff with egg noodles, making pureed squash, chopping cucumber for a salad, baking challah bread, and slowly stewing a mixed fruit compote for dessert: my father's favorite dinner.

As much as I was happy they made up, I was confused and angry, too. I thought my father was mean to my mother, and I thought my mother was too nice to my father. It was a lot to try to process in my young brain.

Our parents are the first relationship we witness as children, and because we're impressionable and emotionally underdeveloped we'll learn from them and mimic their behavior even if we find it offensive and swear we'll never be like them.

I also began to catch on to how masterful my parents were at creating the appearances they wanted others to see. My mother would clean the house for days before a dinner party and even hire a cleaning lady to help. The way they interacted with company was gracious. No one suspected what happened behind closed doors.

When I got older, I understood why my parents resented each other. They stayed in an unhappy relationship, believing they had no other options than to stay together for their children. They were married for sixty-five difficult years. My father died suddenly while sitting in a hot tub. At the end of her life, my mother suffered from severe dementia and lived in the memory care unit of an assisted living facility.

They both lived their lives for appearance's sake, not from their hearts and souls that held their true needs and desires. Knowing this saddens me deeply because they deserved to live a great life.

I became very much like my mother as I got older in that I acquiesced in my relationships. I became a People Pleaser early on by watching my mother modeling the behavior. The difference was in our expressions. My mother was welcoming. I just wanted everyone to go away. I became resistant and angry, especially the more I did for others at my expense. I shape-shifted into what was expected of me. Early on, I knew on some level that I was living a lie.

People-Pleasing was a great choice back then. And because it was effective in childhood and helped me to survive, it continued throughout my adulthood.

Think back to your childhood and remember the ways your parents related and behaved. Allow yourself to see the similarities with the qualities in your expression even if it's different from theirs.

Imagine that by watching their behavior you took in the messages or lessons they were trying to teach you. Notice how you carried these in your life. For example, my mother had taught me that it's better to be nice and do your best to make others happy than to set boundaries. She also taught me to allow men to call the shots as she did with my father.

Look for the ways your family presented themselves to the outside world. Consider the discrepancies between what went on behind closed doors and how your family presented itself to the outside world. Reflect on how you show yourself to the world based on these experiences. We all wear personas. People Pleasers are always *"on"* using enormous amounts of effort to receive favorable attention from others. People Pleasers own the persona that's good, nice, and always available to lend a helping hand.

CHAPTER 4

SACRIFICING YOUR NEEDS AND DESIRES
TO PLEASE OTHERS

Be there for others, but never leave yourself behind.

~ Dodinsky

"Can we stay here for a while?"

My big, brown eyes gazed at Ana pleading for her to help us. She opened the door in her floral house dress. Her thick, black hair lay haphazardly along her face. She had an olive complexion which gave away her Italian descent. Beads of sweat had settled around her nose, and I could hear the vacuum cleaner running in the background.

Ana looked down at us. She was a short, stout woman. At our tender age of five, we looked up at her.

"My beautiful babies!" she said. "What are you doing here? Does Mommy know where you are?"

"We've run away," I said. I held the strap of my Barbie suitcase with one hand while holding my sister's hand with the other. She carried a small satchel.

To this day, I don't know what prompted our decision to run away. I can only assume that my parents' craziness was the culprit and that we felt trapped enough to want to escape.

Ana took us in, sat us down, and served us some spaghetti. While we ate, I could hear Ana on the phone. "Yes, Lilly. They say they ran away."

I remember my mother running in the door a short time later and summoning us home. We had frightened her, and she threatened to tell our father when he returned home that night.

There were no more escape missions for Judy and me after that. I can't speak for my sister, but I understood that scaring my mother wasn't a good idea. After this event, I became quiet and withdrawn. I see our attempt at running away as, most likely, the point when I decided to become a good girl and make my parents happy.

The messages we get as children support us in finding ways to survive. I realized early on that speaking up or challenging the ways I was being treated weren't discussions I could win. So, I chose to become quiet and invisible instead. I took on a lot of my mother's ways of being even when it didn't feel right. And when I was getting praised for being quiet and staying out of the way, I felt acknowledged and loved enough to keep stuffing down my self-expression.

I refer to People-Pleasing as the Common Behavior because I believe many of us suffer from this sabotaging behavior that's taught, modeled, and even encouraged (to some degree) in our lives. Since most of us look outside of ourselves for love and happiness, it makes sense we're not fully true to ourselves and not completely trusting of our choices and decisions. When we remain disconnected from ourselves, and as long as approval comes from the outer world, People-Pleasing will prevail. As long as our self-image is negative, we'll continue to manipulate our circumstances especially where we feel we have no control. Being disconnected and using old behavioral schemes that have outlived their usefulness is why toxicity shows up when we're adults.

In our early childhood, People-Pleasing was a good survival tactic because we were trapped and at the mercy of our caretakers. It worked wonders back then. The problem is that at some point, many of us abandoned our identity, our self. Eventually, we ceased to exist as individuals and chose to become powerfully invisible instead. We become attuned to everyone else's feelings and emotions and neglect our own. This childhood method of protection, if unaddressed, will persist throughout our adulthood. I can say with conviction that it's wreaked havoc in my life and relationships. Extreme cases become codependent. I have many clients who can't identify their feelings when asked without going into stories about what the other person thinks, feels, or does.

Whatever set us off on the road to insecurity, we made the unconscious decision to People Please to be loved and accepted. Over time, our behavior became a habit and later an addiction. Because the self becomes invisible, People-Pleasing may not feel like it's a choice. Even when we try to make ourselves the priority, when the self is abandoned there's no one to come home to.

Because this behavior supported us early, and since we're no longer concerned about our own needs and wants, we unconsciously continue doing the same things *even when we see later that it doesn't work*. We do what we know. We continue to believe that if we do more and try harder, sooner or later we'll get what we want and need.

The irony is that the same People-Pleasing behavior used to hide insecurity guarantees a high degree of self-loathing that locks in the addiction and has us fixed on the proverbial gerbil wheel. We stay stuck because we're detached from ourselves. Making changes isn't an option because deep within our psyches the message is loud and clear: *We're not worth it.*

CHAPTER 5

COMPROMISES, VIOLATIONS, AND REPEAT OFFENDERS

Never compromise yourself. You're all you've got.

~ Janis Joplin

"When will you be home?" asked my husband, Daniel, who was at the top of the stairs.

It was mid-morning, and the sun was streaming through the window. I stood at the bottom of the stairs with a few of my favorite clothes draped over my arm. He was still in his sleeping attire: boxer shorts and a white undershirt, appearing taller than his six-foot, four-inch-frame as he stood looking down at me. His dark brown curly hair looked coifed, and his rosy cheeks gave the impression he was in perfect health.

"I don't know," I said. "I'm going to the cleaners, taking Ashley to the groomer, and running some errands."

I was terrified and hoped he wouldn't notice. I could feel myself shaking. I never considered myself to be a good actress, but by the end of this day I should have been nominated for an Academy Award. I lied my way through this day in ways I never knew I was capable of doing. My escape had to go off without a hitch. I felt unsafe with all the unpredictable drama that had manifested in my relationship. Daniel was becoming undone, and I was losing control.

"Let me take some clothes in for you," I said.

Daniel gathered his laundry together and brought it down.

I had been People-Pleasing my way through this marriage. Many times I had to hide how I felt or what I had planned to do on a given day. Daniel was verbally and mentally abusive, and it was easier for me to acquiesce, agree, and accommodate him. On this day, I planned to make big changes in our relationship. It was up to me; I knew no one would come to save me.

Daniel went back into the bedroom, and I headed to the garage. I put the laundry in the trunk of my car and secured my Yorkshire Terrier in her doggie seat. I quickly went back upstairs and into our master bedroom. The shades were drawn, and the television was on. I put my ear up to the closed bathroom door and could hear the shower running. I didn't have much time.

I laid down on the floor beside our bed and reached my hand underneath it on his side. I reached until I felt it. Daniel insisted on keeping the shotgun for protection. It was about four feet long and secured in its case. I carefully slid it out and left the bedroom silently. Back in the garage, I carefully put it into the trunk. I then slid into my seat, breathed a sigh of relief, and headed out.

My first stop was at the bank where I withdrew enough money to get by for a while. I dropped Daniel's clothes off at the cleaners and asked them to call Daniel when they were ready for pickup. I left the shotgun with my parents.

As I headed down the highway toward New York City, I felt courageous, powerful, and hopeful. I boarded Ashley at a reputable doggie hotel and then headed to my sister's apartment on the Upper East Side. I had only one more thing to take care of: to call Daniel to say I was leaving him.

Just two days before, I had dinner with my parents in an Italian restaurant that we frequented often. The dimly lit room had soft music playing, and you could hear the sounds of utensils as the patrons ate their meals. I had barely touched my chicken parmigiana when I cleared my throat, took a sip of water, and began talking.

"Daniel got mad while we were in the car the other day. He stepped on the gas and floored it down the hill on to Route 9! It was a miracle we weren't killed!" I paused and then added, "I'm very afraid for my life!"

My parents were skeptical and didn't believe me. They didn't think my husband was capable of violence. They remained calm and continued eating, while I described the latest traumatic situation.

My mind screamed, "Isn't this where they insist I come home with them and leave this man?!"

It took every ounce of energy to fight back my tears. Their lack of reaction sparked confusion and sadness in me. I excused myself and headed to the ladies' room when my right foot slipped out from underneath me. I landed flat on my back. At that moment, I wished I could stay there forever.

Four waiters ran over and helped me up. By the time I reached the bathroom, I couldn't hold back the tears any longer and began to sob uncontrollably. Moments later, I looked in the mirror. And that's when I knew what I needed to do. No one was coming. No one would help me. It was up to *me* to save me.

Daniel was sleeping when I returned home. I sat at my kitchen table and closed my eyes. That's when I had a vision of my family huddled at my gravesite. They were crying. That image shook me to the core. I knew I'd reached my tipping point; I'd had enough.

I cuddled up on the couch in the family room and made plans for the next morning. At daybreak, I started my plan's execution and rehearsing the story I'd tell my husband so I could get out of the house safely with my dog, Ashley.

I picked up the telephone in my sister's living room and dialed home.

"Hello." Daniel picked up the phone on the third ring.

"Daniel, it's me. Please listen carefully." I took a deep breath then continued.

"I'm not coming home, and I'm leaving you. Please feel confident that I don't want to make any trouble for either one of us, but in return, I request the fastest, quickest, and fairest divorce that ever transpired in the state of New York."

"Who is this?" Daniel demanded.

"Are you kidding me? It's me, Eve," I said. "Who do you think it is?"

"Eve wouldn't do this."

"She would, and she is!" I shouted.

I heard Daniel in the background choking and making sounds that had me worried he wasn't handling this well. He had a way of getting me to back down and give in to him by acting in dramatically obsessive ways to scare me and tug at my heartstrings. It wasn't going to work this time. I didn't want anything bad to happen, and I was worried. But more important, I was scared for myself and just wanted out. I hung up the phone.

I stayed with my sister for the next month relaxing and getting my bearings. Daniel traveled out of town to see his family and bombarded me with flowers, letters, and phone messages promising to seek help and change. Against my better judgment and that of professionals too, I accepted his pleas and returned to the marriage. I believed his promises would stick. For another two years, I endured more heartache and was physically exhausted by the time it did end.

Along with my People-Pleasing behavior, I became a Repeat Offender. I returned to a relationship that was compromising and violating after I had summoned the courage to leave. I betrayed myself. I didn't set boundaries or stand my ground. Instead, I allowed the relationship to further whittle away at my self-confidence. I continued People-Pleasing, and predictably, I became more disconnected from myself. Finally, I ended the relationship but only after I became terrified of staying one more day. In the end, I believed that he would kill me or I would die much too young of natural causes. It was only two more years, but I now had additional scars to carry with me.

What I know for sure is that we can only change ourselves. When we compromise and violate ourselves through our relationships, we're diminishing our opportunity for a happy life. As much as we'd like things to work out, when we're attached to a particular outcome, we're attempting to manipulate circumstances we have no control over.

People-Pleasing behavior has repeat offenses built right into it. People-Pleasing, *by its very nature*, continues to compromise and violate the self which leads into repeat offenses. When we continue to repeatedly offend it becomes harder to make the changes that will take us to a better life. It also prevents us from learning and heeding the lessons our challenges are bringing to us and gaining the wisdom we need to better ourselves and live peacefully.

- How have you been a Repeat Offender?
- Are you presently in relationships with people who have hurt and betrayed you?
- Have you failed to set boundaries with people who take no responsibility for their actions and behaviors and continue to People Please to keep the relationship together?
- Have you allowed yourself to be abused by others over and over again to remain in a relationship even if it doesn't feel good because you're afraid of being alone?

My client, whom I've named Stephanie, is another example of a Repeat Offender. Stephanie's fiancée called off their wedding a few weeks before the event. Not once, but twice!

Stephanie met Jordan on a popular dating site, and they hit it off almost instantly. Their relationship moved very quickly, and within three months, Jordan proposed to Stephanie. She said yes instantly without knowing Jordan well. She was in for a series of surprises.

Jordan had been married four times before and was receiving alimony from his latest ex. When Stephanie and Jordan moved into the house that Stephanie owned, Jordan convinced her to refinance the property and add his name. Even though her family and friends tried to talk her out of doing this, she went ahead anyway. She acquiesced even though she had mixed feelings about it. She wanted Jordan to know how much she cared about him.

They set their wedding day for the spring. A few weeks before the wedding, he got cold feet and asked if they could postpone for a year. As upset as Stephanie was, she did what Jordan asked. One year later, and only two weeks before the rescheduled wedding, Jordan said he couldn't go through with it.

Stephanie asked Jordan to move out of the house. He refused. So, she moved in with a friend. She had grown uncomfortable around him, and his unpredictable mood swings had become too much for her to bear. Jordan fought being evicted, so Stephanie paid legal fees she could barely afford to force him out. She felt ashamed about having to take legal action to reclaim her home and that her People-Pleasing ways created chaos in her life.

Stephanie is a People Pleaser and an extreme Repeat Offender. When she had clear evidence that Jordan wouldn't commit to the relationship the first time, she continued to compromise and violate herself and her values by acquiescing and accommodating to Jordan's wishes. By the time she came to me for support, she was emotionally devastated, and her self-confidence was at an all-time low. She felt stuck everywhere in her life and didn't think she could pull herself out of the deep hole she'd fallen into.

Had Stephanie decided to end the relationship after the first wedding was called off, she may have secured the confidence and courage she needed to gain her resolve, heal, and move on. Instead, against her better judgment, she continued to allow herself to experience the same heartbreak all over again.

Today, Stephanie is thriving. She lives in a new home, is in a new relationship, and has regained her confidence. She understands that as a People Pleaser she *attracted* a partner whom she allowed to call all the shots. By learning to reform from this destructive behavior, she was able to move on and create a new life and find a new, better-for-her love.

In another example, Gina was being taken advantage of by a group of girlfriends. Because Gina was an avid People Pleaser, she couldn't say no. Every time these women wanted something from her, she managed to come to their rescue.

One day, while having lunch with her friends, Gina overheard one of them having a phone conversation in the ladies' room. Toni, unaware that Gina had entered the room, said, "Gina is such a push-over, and she's boring, too." As Gina listened, Toni continued denigrating her to the other person.

Gina was deeply hurt. She felt betrayed. Instead of letting Toni know she'd heard her conversation, Gina turned and left. Even though Toni had betrayed her, Gina was uncomfortable confronting her. She didn't want to hurt Toni's feelings or embarrass her.

Many People Pleasers feel responsible for *everything* that happens in a relationship because deep down they don't feel worthy, and they blame themselves for problems even if they aren't responsible. In turn, their self-abuse attracts experiences that reflect their low self-worth.

Despite knowing about Toni's two-faced ways, Gina continued the friendship and didn't stop doing favors for Toni. Time passed, and Gina began reading and healing. As she healed, she became angry at herself for continuing to be a friend to these women. One day, she stopped talking to Toni and the other women abruptly. She didn't believe she owed them any explanation. She just wanted to be done. Cutting them off was a powerful step in the right direction for Gina.

To be loved and accepted, People Pleasers repeatedly sabotage themselves (repeat offenses) to make others happy. Continuing this behavior creates toxic relationships and fosters high degrees of self-loathing in People Pleasers. As relationships become toxic, People Pleasers become more insecure and less confident. They begin to question their judgment and decisions keeping them stuck. People Pleasers rely on others to define who they are because they lack the self-validation and acknowledgment everyone needs to thrive. They toil on the victim's path.

CHAPTER 6

ACCOLADES, APPROVAL, ACCEPTANCE, VALIDATION, AND LOVE

The Ache for home lives in all of us. The safe place where we can go as we are and not be questioned.

~ Maya Angelou

Accolades, Approval, Acceptance, Validation, and Love. At some point in my life, around the time I discovered boys and started dating at fifteen years old, I fell into a deep sleep.

My boyfriend, Greg was a six-foot-one Italian god who looked more like a Greek Adonis. His dark brown eyes were mesmerizing, and his golden locks of hair accentuated his striking good looks. It's not surprising I lost my virginity to him in the woods behind the country club my family belonged to.

Greg was popular, and I felt important in his presence. I had the guy all the girls daydreamed about in class. So, I made it my business to make (and keep) him happy so that his focus remained on me.

I believe that was the beginning of the spell I fell under. The sensation of being in love for the first time was intoxicating. It was the beginning of my relationship experience aside from witnessing the union between my parents.

This early experience accentuated my People-Pleasing behavior. Greg was demanding. He needed a lot of attention, and it was his way or the highway. While it felt wrong and unfair that our relationship was like this, he'd give the good talk, telling me how much he loved me, how beautiful he thought I was, and how happy I made him. In those moments, I felt like I belonged.

Our relationship lasted three and a half years. I called it quits after Greg started dating other girls, and I found out about it. I was devastated but refused to continue in a relationship with someone who betrayed my trust. I found the courage to break up with him despite his pleas of being sorry and that he'd do anything to get me back.

Two weeks later, he suffered a near-death motorcycle accident that kept him in the hospital for six months. All of his friends were pleading with me to become his girlfriend again.

"He is sorry, and he loves you," they would say. "How could you not be there for him at such a low time in his life?"

When I went to visit him, his head was pulled back by weights. He was in traction for months like this. Both his legs and left arm were set in full casts, and his right arm was in a sling. I broke down crying and stayed for hours.

My guilt got the best of me and, against my better judgment, I became his girlfriend, nurse, and devoted friend. Within a year, he made a full recovery. He beat the medical odds that predicted he'd never walk again. He fully gained control of his body. You'd never know by looking at him that he'd been in such a bad accident.

I, on the other hand, began drifting further away from the belief that life would work out for me. I avoided taking responsibility for my life and well-being. I didn't study hard, I used food to make me feel better, and continued People-Pleasing to make sure things remained peaceful at home and school. I didn't feel at peace within myself, but I didn't know why. I know now that I went back to Greg out of guilt and because I felt sorry for him. The message I was receiving was loud and clear: I didn't count. Worse, I didn't think I had any control over that.

What keeps us repeating the same behavior *even when we know* we're living a lie on some level? There must be a benefit of sorts that makes us stay in our patterns, even when we know we're headed for a disaster. There must be an agenda if we keep doing things against our will or better judgment.

What feeds a People Pleaser? What's worth sacrificing your needs and desires in the pursuit to make others happy? What keeps you compelled to keep putting in the effort, trying harder, juggling everyone else while abandoning yourself?

Every sabotage pattern and addiction have their superfoods. First, the need to be validated is assuaged by the instant gratification of accolades. Hearing a "Thank you," "You're the greatest!" and "What would I do without you?" can make any People Pleaser blush.

When people nod with approval or let you know you're valuable, it's an instant confidence booster; it feels good. However, the good feeling doesn't last because it comes from outside yourself. True confidence is generated by your love and approval of yourself. People Pleasers don't love themselves. Validation and the acceptance of others, inclusion within a circle of people, and knowing you matter are essential to the feeling that you're a part of something, especially if it's coming from people you admire.

It's imperative that others like and accept us especially when we're young. When we leave our homes and go off to school, becoming part of a group, or having the people we look up to befriend us means the world, especially when we doubt ourselves and our capabilities, which many People Pleasers do.

The superfood of love is what we all strive for. Without love for ourselves, we rely on the love of others to believe we are lovable. And, because People-Pleasing is compromising and violating to oneself, it guarantees that self-love stays way out of reach.

The accolades, approval, acceptance, validation, and love that People Pleasers are hungry for is hardly a conscious process. Instead, it's an obsession and addiction that compels us to act without thinking or questioning the behavior that we're using to get the love we unknowingly push away.

"Someday, you'll marry a man who'll take care of you." That was my parents' mantra, coupled with the fairytales that rocked me to sleep.

My depression confused me because, from the outside, it appeared I lived a sheltered life with all my basic childhood needs met. But when it came to supporting me to discover who I was as a person, there was no guidance. So, I did whatever I could to win my parents' love and have the perfect, happy family I yearned for.

Whenever I took it upon myself to manage my family to bring joy and peace into my home, whether it was entertaining my sister if she was bored, comforting my mother when my father was upset with her, or trying to cheer up my father after a long day of work, my efforts were not for naught. I was acknowledged for being good, quiet, and helpful.

"You were always such a good little girl," my mother often said over the years. "You never ran around like other children or picked things up that didn't belong to you. You were quiet and well behaved." She would gleam whenever she spoke of me in this way.

One day, as an adult, I challenged her.

"Mom, don't you think there is something wrong if a child is too quiet? Did it ever occur to you that maybe something wasn't right with me or that you discouraged my expression?"

I never got anywhere with this subject, because my mother didn't see it or want to take responsibility for it. I believe it was a combination of both. All I know is that as a young child, People-Pleasing paid off for me, and I was able to trick myself into believing that I came from a good, happy, and emotionally healthy family. The accolades, approval, acceptance, validation, and love I felt as a child came when I stayed good and silent, so that's what I did.

I was grateful that my parents were able and willing to pay for my college education. Even so, they lacked encouragement or knowledge in how to support or direct me. With both words spoken and unspoken, the message was loud and clear: "You'll never be able to take care of yourself. Find a nice guy and get married!" When you live in a world believing you can't fend for yourself, every corner you turn is scary.

In my junior year of college, I experienced a devastating betrayal that sent me spiraling into a deep depression and created the path for all my toxic relationships to come. A three-year courtship with a man named Lance I believed I would later marry abruptly ended when I discovered he was cheating on me. I told him I never wanted to see him again. By now, I had a clear sense of feeling unimportant, victimized, and taken for granted. I felt undesirable and deeply rejected.

By my early twenties, I was disillusioned and codependent with others. I relied on people to tell me who I was. The unhealthy bonds of these relationships meant that I couldn't see myself separate and distinct from others. I relied on others to make me happy.

I resorted to drugs and alcohol when I finally bought into my parents' insistence that I couldn't take care of myself. That belief, coupled with not finding that man to take care of me, pushed me over the edge. I stepped up my People-Pleasing ways because by now, I wasn't only neglecting my self-care, I was abusing myself. Sometimes I thought I had a secret death wish.

Each time I began a new relationship, there would be some promising moments of peace and happiness. However, those moments evaporated as the relationship took a dark turn when I'd begin to think that *it won't last*. The better the relationship seemed, the more fear got in the way. I began compromising and violating myself in terrible ways. I'd risk having sex in new relationships without protection or any knowledge of the other person's relationship history. I'd trust whatever I was told.

Hearing a few nice things was enough to have me trust people I knew nothing about. Each time I compromised and violated myself in this way, I grew more doubtful and uncertain about who I was and what my life was all about. It was an unconscious process that brought with it discomfort and pain.

I could be talked into almost anything as a young adult because I was yearning so badly to be loved by another. I never heard the concept of self-love before, my parents didn't model it, and I wasn't privy to any of the healing information I have today.

Misguided praise is what I mean by People Pleaser superfoods, which blind People Pleasers to their harmful dysfunctional behavior, allowing them to continue creating toxic bonds with others all the while deceiving themselves into believing that love is on the way.

Ask yourself the following questions as you begin exposing the ways People-Pleasing feeds you. Notice how justifying and rationalizing this behavior makes sense on some level, even though on many levels you know it doesn't work.

Like any addiction that doesn't serve us, there is a benefit that keeps us compelled to keep repeating the same pattern. Powerful questions will help to reveal what this is.

- When I am asked to do something I don't want to do, what do I say to myself to do it anyway?
- Is it easy for people to convince me to say yes even after I've said no? How? What do they say? What do they do?
- When others ask for favors, am I more likely to say yes if they are complimenting me, telling me how terrific I am, how they can't manage without me?
- Do I feel threatened that if I say no I won't be thought well of, and may even lose them as a friend?

As much as we want to be liked and admired, we must understand and recognize how we manipulate *ourselves* into doing compromising and violating things to ourselves in the process. Our unhealthy relationship with ourselves won't bring us the love we desire. Becoming aware of what influences our behavior is a good first step toward healing.

Chapter 7

The Addiction

There are all kinds of addicts, I guess. We all have pain.
And we all look for ways to make the pain go away.

~ *Sherman Alexie*

Psychology Today defines addiction in this way: "Addiction is a condition in which a person engages in the use of a substance or in a behavior for which the rewarding effects provide a compelling incentive to repeatedly pursue the behavior despite detrimental consequences."

"Do you know there isn't anything I wouldn't do for you? I love you so much!" Matt said earnestly.

A light turned on within me the moment I heard it. I was hopeful again. It all paid off. I'd found him: Mr. Right! I was safe at last and could now exhale. When the man I was about to marry told me this, I believed it with every ounce of my being. It's what I needed to hear to feel secure and to believe I'd be okay. After all, I'd been taught that I couldn't take care of myself by my overcontrolling parents. Plus, I never had positive models to follow. I abandoned myself long ago and felt lost in my life.

Before I was even aware I was doing it, I was searching for someone to take care of me. As a young child, I was neglected emotionally and didn't believe I was worthy. I also took full responsibility for the dysfunction in my family and tried with all my might to manage things. No wonder I got left behind with no one to care for me. It was such a heavy load for such a small person.

I would have been ashamed to admit this in the past, but today I stand tall and without judgment, recognizing that I was desperate and needy. Whether we admit it or not, we all desire and yearn for love and acceptance. If we're not nurtured as children and taught to feed ourselves emotionally as we grow, we'll look for love and acceptance in the wrong—yet familiar—places. It's no wonder many People Pleasers hook up with others who emotionally resemble their family of origin. It's an unconscious way to recreate the traumas of child-hood. We'll continue this behavior until we resolve and bring closure to those traumas.

So, when Matt said those words to me, I believed him. A week later, I felt comfortable enough to ask him to help me clean out my closet. After all, he did say he would do *anything* for me. My request sparked an argument, and we didn't talk for a few days. It clearly showed me his words weren't genuine.

My fantasy kept me going. I was addicted to the hope that I'd be taken care of. My People-Pleasing behavior was delivering the high I needed to keep me committed. I believed deep down that I could make someone love me enough so that they'd devote their time and atten-tion to me. All I had to do was convince them I was lovable. At the time, I didn't know this was what I believed, and I couldn't see how I'd manipulated my circumstances. It was just how I automatically oper-ated. People-Pleasing seemed like the *only* way to get what I wanted.

As needy and desperate as this sounds, I knew deep down that I could be lovable to someone. Even though I didn't feel confident and strong about who I was or what I had to offer, I could be more if I needed to be. I knew there was a part of me that was special. I could remember feeling good about what I had to offer before my relation-ships began to sour.

People-Pleasing was the only way I knew of safely expressing myself while going after what I believed would bring me safety, secu-rity, and happiness. That meant being nice and doing what others needed so they would want to keep me around.

In the last chapter, I covered the superfoods of the People Pleaser. It's safe to say these are incentives to keep us People-Pleasing. It's great to receive some return on our investment, so the instant gratifica-tion of the accolades, acceptance, approval, validation, and love was coveted. But it's the hidden fear that if we don't do for others or make them happy, we'll lose them or have to live with believing that we're worthless and unlovable. So we set out to be more of what we think we *should be,* so we aren't seen for the things we fear we *could be.*

Most people don't realize that many of our choices and decisions are based out of fear. Most of us lack or lose faith that life will work out for us due to one too many disappointments. After experiencing enough loss, we may believe we can't bear to lose anymore, so we make whatever choices necessary to avoid future suffering.

People-Pleasing arises out of insecurity and fear. It may have served us early in life to survive the circumstances we were trapped in, but it's not a healthy, supportive way to live, and it doesn't create satisfying relationships.

People-Pleasing is learned over time. When it becomes the only way we know how to behave, because we've detached from ourselves emotionally, it becomes part of our identity. We become addicted to the promise that this way of being will produce love and acceptance.

We've been tricked into believing that if we do for others, we'll be gifted with appreciation, reciprocation, respect, and love. But People-Pleasing has the opposite result because of its inauthentic, "giving to get" agenda. Our relationships can't move beyond superficiality. People-Pleasing sets us up for the ultimate rejection and helps bring about the self-fulfilling prophecy that no one will love us and we'll be alone. No one can fill us up in the way we need but ourselves. No one but ourselves can save us.

Because we've abandoned ourselves in the pursuit of making others happy, the ability to take care of ourselves—even if we want to—no longer becomes an option. We end up feeling frustrated. We want to make changes, address our needs, and step up our self-care, but it feels even more uncomfortable to focus on ourselves than it does on others. Even worse, we don't know how to focus on our needs. Our desire to care for ourselves is no longer a natural one due to pushing our needs and desires away in service to others deemed more important. We abandon ourselves. No wonder it feels uncomfortable to think about our wants and needs!

If and when we're ready to give to ourselves and reclaim our worthiness, we're still disconnected. We won't know our preferences, interests, needs, and desires, which forces us to think long and hard about what those might be. The whole process can derail if we allow the discomfort of the unfamiliar focus on ourselves to overcome our desire to dig deep. Rationalization and justification will supersede the need to do for oneself, and we resume our normal routine of caring for everyone but ourselves. That discomfort is why it can feel easier and more comfortable to do for others. We need "the fix" of feeling needed again. So, we revert to an old mantra: We don't count.

Reforming from People-Pleasing can feel scary at first. Changing old behaviors can also stimulate a great deal of negativity for being "selfish" from family, friends, and others. We fear being seen in a negative light given our psyche relies heavily on recognition from others.

In the Reform section of this book, I discuss several effective actions you can take to work through your People-Pleasing addiction. If you've been spinning in circles with no real breakthroughs in making yourself a priority, it's because addictions are hard to break.

PART 2

THE URGENCY TO STOP NOW!

Chapter 8

The Dangers of People-Pleasing

*I can't tell you the key to success, but the key
to failure is trying to please everyone.*

~ Ed Sheeran

After my third marriage ended over five years ago, I became, for a while, a slave to my anger. Ending this relationship unleashed a previously unknown rage within me. If it weren't for all the support I surrounded myself with—my coach, my willingness to process my feelings, my desire to heal and move forward—I'm not sure how or where that rage might have been expressed. I knew a part of me had died forever; I needed time to grieve and regain my composure. Instead, I fell into a trance-like state of denial.

I was angry at myself for allowing another heartache in my life, which I swore the last time I would never do. I was ashamed, embarrassed, dumbfounded, and utterly disgusted that I couldn't find the love I was seeking. I didn't know it then, but I now recognize I gave up on romantic love at that moment. I vowed never to date again. Giving up is one of the dangers of People-Pleasing because it shuts you down in many ways, often leaving you without the ability to change or correct your decision. The damage done becomes irreparable.

A year after my divorce was final, I threw a beautiful party to celebrate my moving on. It was also to honor my now ex-husband, whom I finally admitted I didn't like. Being able to acknowledge my dislike was an important step for me. I permitted myself to be okay with not liking someone. Today, I'm not angry, and I embrace the lessons and gifts this man had to teach me. But I still don't like him.

Disliking someone is an uncomfortable feeling for an Empath and a People Pleaser.

After that party, I became a hermit. I spent my time decorating my home in a whimsical, enchanted way that made it even harder for me to leave it. I became disinterested in all the things that I once loved such as being out in nature, enjoying phone conversations with friends, walking on the beach, traveling to great destinations, enjoying long dinners with friends, and entertaining in my home.

I was doing whatever was necessary to protect myself. I stopped exercising for a while and gained fifteen pounds. Like my mother, I used food to comfort me, and I put on a happy face when it was necessary.

By giving myself space and time to heal, I began to understand that People-Pleasing was behind the havoc in my relationships. I jumped for joy at this insight! I knew I was on to something big concerning my healing as well as the healing of my clients.

By its nature, People-Pleasing is self-abusive. Without a relationship with the self, People-Pleasing leads us to believe we're behaving in appropriate ways to reel in love. Our lack of self-love, plus our make-them-happy-at-all-costs nature ensures we'll easily attract the opposite of a People Pleaser: the self-absorbed narcissist. In reality, narcissists aren't complete opposites; they suffer from low self-esteem and a lack of self-love, too. They express their behavior with a "me first" attitude versus People Pleasers who operate with a "you first" attitude.

Once I discovered how negative my self-image was—a truth I hid well from myself and others by wearing the "I have it all together!" persona—I had a starting point to begin my work. I could finally make sense as to why my relationships didn't work. I could finally understand that I attracted people who, despite their different expressions, disliked themselves as much as I disliked me. I could also see how my People-Pleasing ways whittled away at my confidence which caused me to *try even harder*. I was unable to set boundaries with myself or anyone else.

It slowly became apparent that my lack of faith in people and relationships were new dangers I had to face. Consequently, I needed to find my answers quickly so that I could be of service to other People Pleasers by helping them see, understand, and stop their destructive behavior.

I got to work developing an effective process to move away from People-Pleasing behavior that included creating a healthy relationship with myself. Critical to my work was cultivating actions that I could rely on to stick. Today, my friendships are thriving, and I'm no longer in my trance of denial. Even with the scars I carry, I'm creating an extraordinary life for myself. By supporting myself first, I've become a guide in encouraging others to heal and reform. If I can do it, you can do it.

Once you stop People-Pleasing, you can start serving the world. Through the healing process, you'll get to know and bond with yourself and discover what you have to offer. And by taking care of you first, you'll have all you need to impact and inspire people in ways you can't imagine now. That's a win-win for you—and for them.

CHAPTER 9

UNCONDITIONAL LOVE, VULNERABILITY, AND THE BOUNDARYLESS TERRAIN

A little sincerity is a dangerous thing, and a great deal of it is absolutely fatal.

~ Oscar Wilde

"Love means never having to say you're sorry."

Are you kidding me?

This well-known Hollywood catchphrase was made famous in the 1970 movie, *Love Story*, based on the novel by Erich Segal. The story centered around a beautiful, young married couple, Jenny and Oliver, played by actors Ali McGraw and Ryan O'Neal. Their relationship ended when Jenny died from a terminal illness diagnosed after their marriage.

Jenny says this famous phrase to Oliver as he's apologizing for an angry outburst. It's said later in the movie, this time by Oliver after he informs his father of Jenny's death. The relationship between father and son had become strained due to his father's unwillingness to accept Oliver's marriage to Jenny.

I was thirteen when I saw the movie, and I thought it was beautiful. Fantasizing about love and meeting the man of my dreams one day occupied much of my imagination at that age. I can still watch the movie today and use up a box of tissues because love is just a beautiful thing to witness. And, when young lovers are torn apart by something no one can control, it's heart-wrenching.

If we examine this relationship off the Hollywood screen and consider the concept of *unconditional love*, we'll discover how our expectations can impact both People-Pleasing behavior and the lack of boundary setting. Both have a big effect on our relationships.

Jenny is a People Pleaser. She's overly accommodating, overly doing for others, and she barely attends to herself. Even when she gets upset or disagrees with Oliver, she's passive and lacks boundaries in the relationship. When Oliver apologizes for his bad behavior, she deflects it with her one-liner that diminishes his responsibility and eliminates accountability. Even during her illness, leading up to the moment of her death, she was selfless and focused on others.

Today, we hear, "No worries," or "No Problem," as niceties that people use to let others know it's all okay. Consider removing these phrases from your vocabulary because, if you have strong feelings over someone's offensive behavior and you use these to deflect how you feel, you're minimizing your right to an apology and giving the other person the freedom to treat you however they choose. You're enabling bad behavior.

"Love means never having to say you're sorry," sounds like unconditional love. I cried rivers along with everyone else in that theater when Jenny said it. We all yearn to be loved for who we are and crave forgiveness for how we've wronged ourselves and others. But is it realistic to never admit a wrong? Do we ever truly forgive? Is giving a pass to bad behavior healthy or is it giving each person permission to behave badly?

The Wikipedia definition of unconditional love states: "*Unconditional love* is known as affection without any limitations or *love* without conditions."

I believe unconditional love is an unrealistic expectation and an absurd goal. Even if you're surprised reading this right now, if you take some time to think it through it may make some sound sense to you.

Being taught to strive toward unconditional love for all of humanity is a beautiful endeavor, but in reality, it's a fantasy. I believe we can create unconditional love between our creator and us but expecting it between two people sets us up to fail.

Allow me to explain.

Unconditional love lacks boundaries. It can be used as a free pass to treat each other badly. It infers no consequences. And even though we think we're doing it with our spouses, our children, our dogs, and even God, if we're radically honest with ourselves we'll realize we've had temporary setbacks with everyone regarding authentic love. When we're annoyed, exhausted, angry, sad, disappointed, frustrated, and disillusioned with our relationships, we not only *feel* a lack of unconditional love, we *withhold* love from ourselves and others. Not honoring our feelings is a form of self-abuse.

Love means *always* having to say you're sorry. I believe this is a more appropriate practice to strive for if we desire mutually respectful relationships with ourselves and others. There's also a better chance of bringing us closer to the all-loving and accepting world that we seek. By believing that love means always having to say you're sorry, we'd be closer to unconditional love versus sabotaging our chances for it.

If the movie came out today with the same message, I believe a more befitting title would be, "People-Pleasing Can Make You Sick!"

We welcome toxicity into our relationships when we reject boundaries and rationalize our feelings or justify other people's bad behavior while expecting unconditional love. Everything has conditions. If you consider your relationships through this lens, you'll see that what I'm challenging here does make sense, even if you don't want to see it or don't agree with it.

Love can be constant and consistent. We can love others despite what they do. But to say there are no conditions and that we love in every moment is nonsense. I believe the bigger issue is that people aren't honest with themselves about all their feelings. The unconditional love conversation glosses over the negative, hateful feelings that come up. How many times do you hear people throw around the phrase, "I love you," when you know they don't mean it? By honoring our true feelings, especially the negative ones, a deeper love can emerge, one that's authentic and real.

Another trap we set for ourselves is believing the only way to have a deep relationship is by being completely open in our intimate relationships. Believing we should share everything or asking our partner to define who we are is detrimental to relationships that could otherwise be strong and good. Not everything is necessary to share. And allowing someone else to define you can have devastating consequences.

I triggered my client, Tim, during a conversation. He became defensive when I shared these thoughts:

"You're the only person who thinks we share too much," Tim told me after I said that I believe relationships are on the decline because we aim to be too vulnerable and connected. "We're spreading the fear," I declared.

"What do you mean?" he asked. He was curious to know where I was headed, but I could feel his defenses coming up since he'd been told the opposite advice for years.

When Tim entered into a coaching relationship with me, he and his wife benefited greatly. They became closer and were having more fun. A black cloud had lifted off their relationship which had become detached and combative. Through our coaching work together, it became evident that by addressing his healing, Tim was creating the effect he wanted for his relationship. "It's not about the two of you as a couple. It's about the individual and the wounded histories brought into the relationship that causes disharmony in the union," I explained.

"As much as we yearn to be deeply connected with others, especially in our romantic relationships, the desire to be seen has more to do with our individual *need to belong* and *to matter in the world* than it does to connect deeply with another. It's about seeking validation from others that should come from within the self," I said.

Based on my experiences—three failed marriages plus a great deal of inner reflection—I strongly believe we want others to comfort us about our insecurities. We want them to change our minds when it comes to how crappy we feel about ourselves and our lives. It feels good to imagine being vulnerable with others, but when the opportunity arises, it's scary. Too much vulnerability can negatively impact the relationship, kill the passion, and even cause a breakup.

Even though it's nice to think of our spouses as our best friends, lovers, and confidants, there's a fine line that few people acknowledge. We desire to connect emotionally, but we don't stop to think that the depth of that bond could destroy the connection altogether.

In all my marriages, I believed that deep connection was the ultimate factor in recognizing whether a relationship was emotionally bonded. I wanted my husband to get me, to see me, to tell me about me, and to be right about it. I was disappointed when that wasn't the case. Then, believing the relationship was broken, we sought marriage counseling, which I now believe is the fastest and quickest way to end a relationship for good. I firmly believe that sharing deeply in relationships, where there's a personal investment of quality time, money, and especially the heart, is not always wise and I will tell you why.

One morning after making love with my husband, we had a deep conversation. I asked him about his romantic history as we were sharing about our past.

"Most of the time, I wished my girlfriends would leave after we had sex. I couldn't wait to be alone. It was torture," he said.

Now, on the one hand, I felt close to him and was happy that he opened up deeply to me. But I was terrified every time we made love because I couldn't shake what he'd said. It became part of how I saw our relationship.

Imagine this scenario: Your husband runs his own business, and he's scared it won't be successful. He has no basis for his fear such as an impending bankruptcy. He's feeling generalized fear. One night, he decides to confide in you about his fear. While you try to be receptive, he's now spread his fear to you. Now you're both afraid and sending negative energy into the business. My point is this: Consider whether your spouse or partner needs the information you wish to share and how it might affect the relationship. I believe most people fail to realize how detrimental oversharing can be to the success of their relationships. Think before you unburden yourself. Think before you share.

Does the other person need to know or are you simply wanting to share your pain or experience? For a relationship to thrive, there needs to be a positive vision of the relationship.

When we marry, we become more invested in the relationship because we're mixing finances, making purchases such as real estate, and setting the expectation that we're partners for life. It's a huge responsibility, and it's life-altering. It's also better to share information that builds the relationship up instead of tearing it apart. Most couples only communicate when things are going wrong rather than when things are going well. The best time to share is when things are going well!

I'm suggesting that we seek support for our emotional wellness as individuals so that we can address our doubts and fears. We can also join support groups or confide in good friends who care about us but who don't have a personal investment in how our relationships turn out. We all need to vent and gain support around what we're afraid of. That's a healthy thing to do. But when we vent and express our fears to the people in whom we're emotionally invested, we run the risk of changing how they feel about us and the relationship, even if they assure us they understand. As much as we'd like to believe it's a loving gesture to share everything, it's not. Conditions exist in every relationship.

Sadly, many people stay in relationships that make them miserable believing they have no other option. A belief in unconditional love can help us justify and rationalize staying in relationships that don't feel good.

Many people in marriages and intimate relationships often say, "I love him/her, but I'm not *in love* with her/him. I believe this happens not so much with time and routine, but because they believe they must share everything, especially their feelings. Following that advice may give the impression they're deeply in love, but it can also kill the passion quickly.

I don't advise being deceptive. Certain information needs to be shared such as a medical illness, impending bankruptcy, or anything that has to do with a major life change. However, it doesn't make sense, and it will only make everyone uneasy if we share the ordinary, imagined scenarios, doubts, and fears that plague us.

Another instance where speaking up is advised is when someone has done or said something to upset us. We must take responsibility for our feelings; no one can "make" us feel a certain way. So when we're upset over something, it's worthy of discussion, but we still must take responsibility for the things that trigger and upset us. Otherwise, oversharing can create more secrecy and a reluctance to communicate because we won't feel safe to open up in the future.

I believe vulnerability is incredibly courageous. I do believe though, that as much as we say we want it, we're turned off by it when it arrives. If we want to keep our relationship interesting and inspiring then sharing hopes, dreams, and faith will bring us closer together in a positive way.

The journey for all of us is to *know thyself*. It's up to each of us to take responsibility to look in the mirror and meet ourselves. It's not realistic for others to show us who we are. It is our sole responsibility to bond with ourselves.

I'm deeply saddened by the statistics of marriages that break up. I believe that many can thrive. When we take responsibility for ourselves and build our confidence we can relate more effectively with others.

Here's a conversation I had with my second-husband-to-be early in our relationship that supports this recommendation:

"Promise me we'll never have to impress each other," Brad said while looking at me.

His blue eyes were mesmerizing as he held me in his arms. I felt safe, secure, and loved. And then, BAM! The excitement was sucked right out of me. I wiggled my way out of his embrace.

"What do you mean?" I demanded. "Don't you think love is about always impressing each other?"

Little did I know then that my relationship with Brad was predictable, given his comment and how differently we saw things. Today, it's clear to me that I was the People Pleaser attracting the narcissist and that it would all play out very toxically. It was telling as well about the lies and betrayals to come and lackadaisical ways of non-connecting.

Relationship boundaries have more credence when they're set at the beginning of a relationship as things arise. Setting boundaries later can be more difficult especially if a lack of respect is present and the People-Pleasing partner doesn't feel taken seriously.

Brad and I married a year later and, as predicted, our relationship didn't last; we divorced eighteen months later. We both stayed true to our perspectives and before long, his perspective won. I had stopped caring, and no one was putting in the effort to impress the other. We called it quits.

I didn't recognize that my People-Pleasing ways made no room for boundaries because the behavior is so contradictory to respect within a relationship. I also missed the destruction that People-Pleasing caused in my life because I was in denial and pointing my finger at everything and everyone but me. I believed it wasn't my fault. I didn't know what boundaries were, much less how to set them. What I did have clarity about was that I was miserable, and I didn't feel loved. I dwelled in the confusion of why someone as nice as me was attracting people who weren't so nice. I wasn't aware of my poor self-image or that my actions were bringing about negative experiences.

Today I understand my insecurities and how my relationships lacked the boundaries needed to set the foundation of trust, respect, and responsibility firmly in place. People Pleasers don't set boundaries because they lack self-love and respect. They sacrifice their needs and desires. Without self-respect, they can't set boundaries. It's worse if they're also codependent.

People Pleasers may confuse their anger and frustration for boundary setting when they react or confront others with their displeasure. Unfortunately, all that's happening is a rant that makes them appear irrational or overly sensitive. In the end, many People Pleasers take all the blame for what's happened. Doing so is a sure way to create more negative self-talk and continue doing more for others.

To set boundaries, they must trust themselves, be clear about their needs and desires and be able to convey them to others in a confident, assertive manner. Remember, People Pleasers are disconnected from themselves and because they can't trust themselves; they are full of self-doubt and trepidation. Setting boundaries is a mystery to People Pleasers even though they know on some level they want to stand their ground.

It took another marriage for me to get and heed this lesson. When I got it, I got it in spades! I had a lot of reflecting to do.

Remember Matt in chapter one, the prince who woke me up to me? That relationship was my first real lesson on setting powerful boundaries. I knew my marriage to Matt was over. I just wasn't sure how to proceed with the divorce and living arrangements. My history of exits had more to do with getting out as fast as I could even if I traveled light and without the things I was entitled to have. I had screwed myself more than once.

This time, I wanted it to be different. One day, I sat in my office contemplating my options. I closed my eyes and became conscious of my breath as I imagined my past behavior as a guide to this situation. Then, I opened my eyes, took another breath, and closed them again. I imagined staying in our house together for as long as it took to get what I was entitled to and setting the needed boundaries that were screaming in my head and body.

Physiologically, I felt stronger and more at peace taking the boundary path. I had a lot of built-up disappointment and anger, and I needed to act on it instead of pushing it away or acting it out. It was time to grow up and take care of me. I felt confident and inspired.

Even though I was in the process of ending a relationship, I felt powerful. I was bonding with myself by applying the essential ingredient in my recipe for healthy, successful relationships: boundary setting. Learning to do this was the cure-all for much of my People-Pleasing ways that had previously sabotaged the love I always wanted.

"I have a proposition for you," I told Matt as I invited him to sit in our living room.

By this time, we'd both agreed our divorce was inevitable. The next step was setting the logistics of a separation agreement and moving on.

"I have a solution that I believe will work for both of us," I told him.

He listened closely, and I could see the tears well up in his eyes as I shared how we should divide things.

When I was finished, he rose from the couch, sat down next to me on the loveseat, and hugged me. "I thought we were both going to be ruined financially after this. Thank you," he said.

"That's not what I want for either of us," I insisted.

We exchanged a sincere smile that was a long time coming. I felt things would be okay for both of us and that moving on was the right choice.

As Matt began to climb the stairs to his office, I called after him.

"Matt, when you speak to your lawyer, remember it's not negotiable. If this settlement is changed in any way I won't agree to it. He looked down at me from the top of the stairs and nodded.

"What's going on?" Jill, my lawyer, asked in a phone call. "The terms of this Settlement Agreement aren't at all what we discussed," she said. "I sent you an email. Review it and call me back."

I quickly opened my email, read the revised agreement and placed a call to Matt.

Matt picked up on the second ring. "Hello?"

"Matt, I was sent the revised agreement that your lawyer drafted. We didn't agree—"

"What part don't you like?" he demanded, cutting me off.

"Deal's off!" I shouted and hung up the phone.

It was now clear that being nice to Matt wasn't such a good idea. I should've known as much, since leaving this marriage accounted for the nice guy being not so nice. For the first time, I recognized how my People-Pleasing ways weren't supporting me or appreciated by others.

"Isn't this the same man who'd cried and hugged me two days ago when I proposed a very fair settlement for the both of us?" I remember thinking.

It was time to change things up.

Four months later, a deal was struck, and it was much better for me than what my original terms outlined, including riders attached to give me extra protection. Matt continued to sabotage himself by thwarting my kindness and even reneged on an important part of the agreement, forcing me to take him to court. For Matt and his attorney's efforts, the judge granted me punitive damages and insisted Matt pay my legal fees for not cooperating. Through it all, I found strength I didn't know I had, and I learned how to be forceful—something People Pleasers don't want to be. Afterward, I had gained confidence, internalized the fact that I had rights, and wasn't intimidated by the demands of my narcissistic partner any longer.

It's essential to know yourself to know your boundaries. If you're People-Pleasing, you're treading on a barren terrain. It's time to open your eyes not only to the way others treat you but how you enable the offensive behavior. People-Pleasing allows others to take advantage of you. When you don't set boundaries, you contribute to the failure of the relationship or to staying where you're just unhappy.

Wikipedia defines personal boundaries as "guidelines, rules or limits that a person creates to identify reasonable, safe, and permissible ways for other people to behave toward them and how they will respond when someone passes those limits."

Consider the following questions:

- Are you in relationships that lack boundaries?
- Do you feel entitled to speak up for what you want and need?
- Do you enable others to treat you badly?
- Do you feel unheard?
- Are you angry that people don't respect or appreciate you?

Asking yourself questions is a great way to gain insight into your relationships. You're the only one who can teach people how to treat you. First, you must care for yourself and model this behavior to others. You must speak up and voice your preferences, dislikes, deal breakers, and other boundaries so the people in your life have a clear picture of you and how to treat you. How others see and treat you has always been up to you.

I suggest you start complaining to gain clarity around the boundaries you want to set by keeping an *it's not okay* list. On that list, write down all the things that bother, trigger, frustrate, sadden, aggravate, disappoint, anger, and annoy you. Don't beat yourself up doing this; just come up with a clear list about the offensive behaviors you won't tolerate. Once you become aware and acknowledge what you have discovered, you can begin to make changes and set boundaries.

Patience and tolerance will be necessary to go through this process because you've enabled people for a long time. Don't expect the other person to change. Just because you've changed, doesn't mean they will. But you must stand your ground. Your relationship was based on who you were when you met. If you choose to reform your People-Pleasing behavior, the dynamic of the relationship will change, and your relationship may be bumpy for a time. For your relationship to have the best shot at being healthy and intimate, boundaries are the way to go.

If you're unhappy in your relationship, your partner probably is as well. I've never heard of one person being blissfully happy and the other person being completely miserable. If you're unhappy, you must open your eyes to see your partner's discontent and unhappiness, too. I also believe the number one factor in most relationship breakups is a better opportunity comes along for one of the parties involved. It's easy to make excuses and follow something more attractive when you're miserable. Just know that if it's easy for you, it might be easy for your partner, too.

CHAPTER 10

ELEVEN GREATEST COSTS OF PEOPLE-PLEASING

Your need for acceptance can make you invisible in this world.

~ Jim Carrey

People-Pleasing comes at a cost. We suffer when we allow ourselves to act in ways that sabotage our lives and relationships. People-Pleasing...

1. Allows for only superficial connections with others because it's inauthentic.
2. Sacrifices your needs and desires so you can't be happy.
3. *Gives to get* with little to no return on investment due to its selfish, self-absorbed behavior.
4. Promotes self-loathing and disconnection from the self.
5. Relies on others to define and validate you so you remain at the mercy of others.
6. Attracts narcissists and offensive behavior.
7. Leaves you frustrated, exhausted, and angry, and increases your risk of major illnesses.
8. Diminishes the opportunity to know yourself and find your purpose.
9. Creates self-doubt and a lack of faith in love that makes you believe you should be alone.
10. Causes you to blame others and withhold love from them and yourself.

11. Makes you believe others' dreams are your own which causes you to live a life unrealized.

I often wonder if any of the above is worth it even if it was possible to make everyone happy. I strongly doubt it. What I don't doubt is that on your journey to know yourself and your place in this world, you've been taught you must sacrifice yourself to be loved. Absurd!

I refer to this as the Essential Misguidance. We innately desire to be there for others, believing our purpose is to serve others and create a better world. But if we sacrifice ourselves in that journey, we have nothing to give. We must do for ourselves first so that we can effectively be there for others and deliver our contribution.

No matter who we are and what we endure on our journeys, we'll find peace if we can make sense of the life we've lived. If we understand our challenges, we'll recognize our triumphs. People-Pleasing discourages this process.

There's no greater tragedy than living your life disconnected from yourself. You won't bond with yourself, know your soul, or discover your purpose in the world. It will create deep sadness and frustration in your life and relationships. It will rob the world of your talents and contributions. We all want to matter and leave our imprint behind. If we didn't then we wouldn't do the things we do to get what we want or be preoccupied with our aspirations in life. Wanting to matter is innate in the human condition. Even before you were emotionally developed or understood the deeper meaning in life, you just knew you needed to matter.

We all seek meaning, whether it's through a vodka bottle or a radical reinvention. That meaning is attainable when things make sense. It's that simple. We may reach a place in our lives when we understand what's going on and how things connect. But we can just as easily fall back and lose faith when things become challenging, confusing, or seem unfair. Allow me to illustrate my point.

When I connected myself (the Common Denominator) to how I was People-Pleasing (the Common Behavior), I realized that the very things I was doing to bring about love were pushing it away. It made sense when I realized that my insecurities had me act in ways that were needy and desperate. It was evident in my past choices when I examined them later. People-Pleasing was whittling away my confidence and increasing my wrath for myself. I could understand why my relationships were disappointing and dysfunctional.

Each time I learned something, gained confidence, or felt inspired, it didn't last because my People-Pleasing behavior continued making any growth seem fleeting. People-Pleasing ensures you stay out of integrity with yourself and that your self-loathing continues to increase.

Humans are wired to look for what's wrong, which is why negativity is far more powerful than positivity. People-Pleasing is destructive, and it diminishes our strength. We continue our behavior because our lack of bonding with ourselves allows for no other choice than putting others first. We don't matter. Our insecurities keep us People-Pleasing, which makes us loathe and disregard ourselves. And then we step up our behavior believing we're just not doing enough. Voilà! Our repetitious behavior is why we're on the gerbil wheel and can't get off!

You must acknowledge the costs of People-Pleasing because you'll need every ounce of willingness, commitment, and effort to stop. Fear can be a great motivator for action, so my intention in this book is to be a compassionate slap in the face and scare you a bit. Humans tend to steer toward safety by nature. People-Pleasing isn't safe. If you recognize that People-Pleasing won't bring you the love you need and desire, then use that danger as your motivation to stop.

The first step is to make sense of the life you've lived. Some people use the metaphor of putting the pieces of a puzzle together. I invite you to find clarity in this way:

When I was a little girl, I had many coloring books. I became obsessed with the pages that displayed a series of dots on a page. Each dot had a corresponding number, and I would love to draw the lines connecting the numbered dots. Little by little I could see a form taking shape. In the end, it became clear. A horse! A flower!! A wagon! I was elated that this page of speckled dots formed something meaningful in a short amount of time.

In the same way, I connect my experiences to form something clear and tangible. For example, connecting the dots on my journey of dissatisfying and toxic relationships led me to discover my low self-worth and People-Pleasing behavior. When I chose to use these experiences as self-improvement tools, I recognized that all the challenges I had experienced supported my growth and evolution to become the person I'd always wanted to be: a responsible adult who can take care of myself and experience love in the world.

Today, I bond with myself more deeply every day, and it's an honor and privilege to be able to support my clients and my readers, too. When you recognize that your journey has been an adventure, leading you directly to your purpose, you'll dance like no one is watching. That's when you'll know what it feels like to *matter*.

If you're willing to take on this perspective, you'll have profound clarity on how you operate and why. To do this work, you'll have to remove any negative judgment about what you'll find and have to add the curiosity and fascination needed to inspire you to uncover your life patterns.

When you begin to connect the dots of your journey, you'll be delighted to find that even your greatest hardships serve a purpose. You'll have a greater appreciation for all that you've lived and all that you've survived. Connecting the dots of your journey means understanding that everything happens for a reason and being able to see your life from a range of vantage points will support this.

It's worth noting that your perceptions and interpretations about what you've seen and experienced were accurate *from your vantage point*. You harbored self-doubt because other people were standing at different vantage points and saw things in opposition to yours. They were right, too.

To heal and make positive changes in your life, you must feel one hundred percent validated as a human being who's lived through drama and trauma and that you deserve to be loved and happy. You can change your life at any moment you decide, provided you're willing to take the steps.

Sometimes people are stubborn and righteous because they can't be wrong about one more thing. It's less about hanging on and more about not wanting to let go of what makes sense to us. It's why others' perspectives can seem like nonsense; the vantage points are different. Stay true to your vantage point, not to remain a victim, but to honor your experience and willingness to move forward from it.

The journey begins with our childhood, our earliest vantage point. As children, we're emotionally underdeveloped. We also encounter new experiences frequently, many that we don't initially understand. To counter our lack of understanding, we create meaning based on what we know at the time. That's how we become locked into believing only those things of which we could make sense. That surety of understanding can become problematic in adulthood.

Joanie is an example of a person whose early vantage point was so chaotic and dysfunctional that she convinced herself it didn't affect her negatively.

"I've been asked by my publisher to write the true story of my life—the one I haven't told yet," she informed me during a session.

I saw this as good news since I had also been encouraging her to begin processing the full story she hadn't yet recognized, despite having already written two books about her life.

Joanie is an unusually brilliant woman who has set very high standards for herself, and against all odds, set out at a young age to chase after her dreams. Despite coming up against huge obstacles that put her life in danger, she moved forward with the force of a bull.

Joanie didn't think of herself as a People Pleaser because she says she's not a pushover, a behavior that many People Pleasers exhibit. Joanie sees herself in a positive light and glosses over her challenging experiences that most of us would question whether we could survive such ordeals. Her view of herself makes her blind to many of the People-Pleasing behaviors that aren't as obvious.

Many People Pleasers live in denial of painful realities because going into the past is too dark and scary. As we age, however, our denial breaks down. Sooner or later the boogeyman from our childhood is going to jump out. It already has many times in Joanie's life. And somehow, someway, Joanie manages to put the blinders back on.

People-Pleasing promotes self-loathing and disconnection to the self. We lose our true expression when we negate who we are and set out to become someone else. We build a persona that resembles someone whom we desire to be. The problem is we abandon who we are for a persona that never feels comfortable. It's like wearing tight shoes or clothes that are itchy and uncomfortable.

Joanie has created a strong persona and doesn't realize how she's given up on the innocent little girl who felt she wasn't good enough. That little girl became overlooked and forgotten for the hard, "No one can hurt me," imposter needed for her to become successful in the cutthroat recording industry. I believe that once Joanie reconnects with her innocent inner child and accepts that little girl as her authentic self, she'll soften and become even more successful in a humble, balanced, and healthy way.

When Joanie fully believes from the depths of her heart that she's a beautiful, worthy, innocent soul, she'll shine more brightly as the talented singer and recording artist that she is. She'll also help many others who have struggled to heal by using the challenges from her journey. Then she'll know what it means to matter. She just needed to connect her dots.

As much as Joanie will continue to rejoice in the accolades and approval of others, she won't need others to validate her life anymore. She'll feel free to share herself fully with the world and have a newfound respect for herself that will hold her in a loving embrace.

Jim is a handsome, well-educated, financial genius who started his own company to help others seek financial freedom and peace of mind. When I asked Jim to share his greatest fear, he told me, "I'm afraid of being discredited."

It's common for all of us to have unrealistic fears that come up at certain times in our lives. As you begin to connect the dots of your journey, you'll discover that beliefs formed after painful experiences are the genesis of nearly every fear we harbor into adulthood. Anything we fear has happened already, that's why we fear it so intensely. We've already had an ample taste of the pain and discomfort, and we want to prevent it from ever happening again.

When Jim was nine, he had a third-grade classmate named Lauren who had some learning challenges in class. Her parents met with the principal and some teachers because they were considering getting Lauren some additional support. The principal suggested Lauren's mother, Susan, speak to some of the other children to see if they can shed any light on how Lauren participates in class.

Susan approached Jim and some others students individually. One day after class, she pulled Jim aside and asked him to share with her what he thought about Lauren.

"Do you think Lauren participates?" she asked.

Jim nodded and wondered why she was asking him questions.

"Do you think she's slow and stupid?" Susan got right to the point.

Jim shook his head no. But Susan kept on insisting that Lauren was slow and stupid, and was badgering Jim to chime in.

Wanting to accommodate an adult and be a good boy, he finally agreed with Susan that yes, Lauren was slow and stupid. Jim, now feeling comfortable in the conversation, added some other details that revealed he thought Lauren wasn't very smart either. They shared a laugh, and Jim went off to meet the school bus and head for home.

The next morning, Jim was called into the principal's office and reprimanded for saying bad things about Lauren. He was told to write a letter of apology to Susan. His parents were also informed, and they punished him by taking away his favorite television show for a week.

Jim was confused. The incident with Susan and the aftermath changed who he was.

Where he once thought he was doing what was asked of him and helping out, he was instead made out to be bad and wrong. Jim was discredited at the innocent age of nine at the hands of an adult who was inappropriately feeding him the answers she wanted to hear.

Looking back, Jim can intellectually understand that Susan was intimidating a child into agreeing with her and that he did nothing wrong. And yet, the profound effect this experience had on him as a child was still reverberating in his life as a mature adult. He was holding back his full expression in fear he would be ridiculed or humiliated.

Jim no longer felt okay after this early event. He became insecure for fear of doing or saying the wrong thing. People-Pleasing behavior seeks assurances that we're okay, so it's no wonder Jim became an avid People Pleaser. But validation from the outside world is never enough. We're the only ones who can fill ourselves up. We must believe we're okay.

Jim understands how he came to be a People Pleaser and has committed to taking the steps toward reforming his behavior. He was able to find many other experiences to support his People-Pleasing ways and is excited to understand how it all began. Jim is bonding with himself more and more every day, and he recognizes that this deep fear was holding him back from expressing himself freely and confidently.

Today, whenever Jim feels someone is out to discredit him, he smiles and hugs the little nine-year-old boy within him who now supports him to stand up for himself and be all that he can be for himself and the world.

By connecting the dots of your experiences, you'll begin to make sense of your journey and understand the fears you have that keep you People-Pleasing. Then, you'll be free to express all of who you are without feeling restricted by others and what they think of you.

CHAPTER 11

TEN GREATEST BENEFITS OF REFORM

Self-reform is the only kind that works.
~ Mason Cooley

Reforming from People-Pleasing has enormous benefits. When we stop the destructive behavior, amazing things begin to happen. By reforming from People-Pleasing you'll...

1. Reunite with your lost self.
2. Bring back good memories from childhood.
3. Have a new respect for yourself and others.
4. Find the courage to let go of the relationships that no longer serve you.
5. Have better experiences and attract better relationships.
6. Be able to forgive yourself and others.
7. Increase your confidence and learn to love yourself.
8. Begin to trust yourself and make higher choices on your behalf.
9. Feel less fearful and go after what you want.
10. Know yourself, discover your purpose, and start serving the world.

When I discovered People-Pleasing was the culprit wreaking havoc in my life, I committed to turning things around. I had no idea what would be available to me as a result. I just knew I needed to stop. I was blown away with all the positive benefits that came my way quickly.

For many years, I was angry with my parents and believed that my childhood was filled with lots of neglect, lack of emotional support, and mental abuse. I wasn't wrong about this, but there were many good memories, too. But they were long ago forgotten. I couldn't recall any.

I firmly believe that our painful experiences stand out and impact our lives much more so than our positive experiences, in part because our wounded psyches are in charge. As noted earlier, we're hardwired to look for the negative, and we tend to hold on to our resentments more tightly. We lose flexibility in the way we see things and become righteous and stubborn, the only path of self-validation for People Pleasers.

When I decided to end my People-Pleasing ways, I was extremely uncomfortable. I had to go against my learned behaviors and change my responses to everything I was doing. Saying no was a challenge. I would ruminate for days. Telling friends and family stories to avoid spending time with them so I could attend to the things I needed to do for myself was hard. I struggled taking care of me.

Because I was so committed and determined, I focused on how I was feeling in every moment. I vowed not to judge anything or make myself wrong for my decisions. I saw this journey as an opportunity to be radically honest with myself and make changes in my life that would bring me joy and peace. Doing this work required me to take responsibility and admit I was wearing a persona that was destroying my chance at real love.

I became super analytical, and it was paying off. One day, I noticed I was resisting feeling anything negative about myself. Because I know that what I resist, persists, I chose to bathe in those dark thoughts. I created a little practice to help me move through my discomfort with more ease. I felt excited and inspired.

The negative thoughts persisted, especially, "Not good enough."

This phrase came up a lot. The feeling that I wasn't enough, it wasn't enough, I wasn't doing enough, I wasn't resting enough. It went on and on until I finally got frustrated and began pulling at my hair. And then I let it out in one loud scream: "Not good enough for *what*!?"

I had a tenfold epiphany at that moment. My process of reforming started with a bang.

I realized that every time I passed a mirror, I'd look to catch a glimpse of myself. I remember being vain most of my life, and appearance was extremely important in my family. If you looked good, you were praised for it. This praise also was evident in the outer world. If people liked your appearance, you were noticed and accepted. Getting older was becoming a challenge.

Many times, I'd look in the mirror expecting to see a woman in her mid-twenties and instead be met with the reality that I'm a woman in my late fifties. Also, I had gained fifteen pounds in the last few years. I could feel my negative judgment coming up singing the chorus of *I'm not good enough*. That's when it hit me. I must be comparing myself to some measurement I've kept in my head.

I sat down at my desk and made a list of all the ways I thought I wasn't good enough. I aimed to be specific, and so my list looked like this:

All Things Not Good Enough

Not pretty enough

Not smart enough

Not educated enough

Not thin enough

Not young enough

Not rich enough

Then I inserted a column next to each 'not good enough' statement so I could answer the question: "Not good enough for what?" Three answers emerged for each statement.

Not Good Enough for What?

Not pretty enough	To be in a beauty pageant
	To be a top model
	To stop traffic
Not smart enough	To go to Harvard
	To enter a spelling bee
	To start a financial company
Not educated enough	To qualify to teach Algebra
	To go for a PhD
	To train medical students
Not thin enough	To wear a string bikini
	To be told, "You're so thin"
	To see my perfect weight on the scale

I began to lighten up as I read my answers. I began to laugh. I even had to make up some outrageous answers because I couldn't come up with rational reasons why I needed to be more of something.

My final column read:

Do you desire to do any of the above, and are they needed to live your purpose?

My answer to all the statements was a resounding *no*!

Whatever I thought I wasn't good enough for, I didn't desire to be. I also didn't need any other qualities or attributes to be the life coach, teacher, and writer I already am. All the things I love to do feed my soul and give me purpose. I already have everything I need. I was elated! I could see that God had given me everything I needed to live a happy life, and all the ways I believed I fell short had nothing to do with my life journey at all.

I feel certain that anything we deeply desire we'll go after. And, if we don't go after it, it's because we don't truly want it. Those desires could also reflect choices other people have for you. People Pleasers commonly live a *should* life, whether it's imposed on them by someone else, or imposed on themselves by doing what they believe is expected of them. Regardless, People Pleasers often live their lives inauthentically and don't desire any of the choices they're given.

I highly recommend you try the above exercise. You may discover that you've set yourself up in ways that keep you stuck and unable to move forward. We get in our way.

This exercise helped me recognize my need for validation and the good feelings I felt when I received it. So, whenever I noticed the *not good enough* feeling creeping up, I recognized it as an old pattern trying to exert its power over me again. I no longer resisted the feeling, but I chose, instead, to honor myself rather than fall into the dark thoughts of my past. For example, if I didn't feel good enough about something, I tended to withhold from myself in some way. If I didn't feel pretty enough, I wouldn't go to the party. If I didn't feel smart enough, I wouldn't attend the network meeting. If I didn't feel thin enough I wouldn't enjoy my meals. It was downright abusive!

My practice changed to give myself everything I could during those insecure times and to step up the ways I could honor myself. If I wasn't feeling pretty enough, I'd acknowledge myself anyway. If I didn't feel smart enough, instead of convincing myself that I was, I'd treat myself as if I was brilliant and special. Whatever it was, I would treat myself as if I was all that—even though I knew I wasn't. I was treating myself well despite my feeling badly.

And guess what? After honoring myself in this way, I didn't need to be whatever I thought I needed to be to feel happy, treat myself well, or enjoy my life. It was eye-opening. The only regret I had was all the time I'd wasted by staying in the dark. And even then, I understood that I wouldn't have reached this epiphany if everything had happened differently.

I needed this learning experience because I could reap the return on investment by committing to change my People-Pleasing behavior. Before long, I didn't need others' approval because I had my own. I also saw that others were respecting me more, going out of their way on my behalf, and wanting to be in my company. I was confident life was turning in my favor.

I even remember being bold enough to say to both my mother and my sister that I loved them but was choosing myself first. My sister now refers to me as "My beautiful sister," and my mother blew me kisses whenever we saw each other. It's uncanny how a positive self-image can make you look more attractive to others.

As you read on, you'll see more practices I implemented to stop People-Pleasing and how these supported me in creating an extraordinary life.

I hope that some of the stories I've shared have resonated with you, and you feel now is the right time to start living the life you desire. I trust that you've had people along your journey who've been rooting for you and saying that you deserve more. Now, it's up to you to leap on your behalf, knowing that my best recommendations are designed to support you in breaking through and getting what you want.

CHAPTER 12

BECOMING YOUR PRIORITY

*Resolve to be thyself; and know that he who finds
himself, loses his misery.*

~ Matthew Arnold

"I didn't like myself," my teacher and mentor said on stage in front of fifteen hundred people. I was a student in a certification course to become a holistic health counselor at the Institute for Integrative Nutrition in New York City. The year was 2006.

Because the room was so large and there were so many people, the two enormous screens at either end of the stage allowed you to see her as if she was right in front of you. My eyes were transfixed on this stunningly beautiful, petite woman dressed in ivory and wrapped in a cashmere shawl. Class and sophistication were the first two words that came into my mind as I watched her.

When she said those four words, the room stopped. I felt a tightness in my throat, and I automatically sat up straight in my chair and stopped taking notes. I was compelled to listen to what this woman had to share.

She doesn't like herself? What's wrong with her? I wondered. All I knew was that if she didn't like herself, she had something to say and I'd better listen. I didn't like myself either. Maybe my struggle with depression would be revealed on this very afternoon. *I'd better open my ears*, I thought.

A year after that talk, I attended her famous three-day "The Shadow Process" workshop. All my negative thoughts became history. I consider Debbie Ford to be the woman who gave me back my life.

The late Debbie Ford was one of the most brilliant people I've ever met. She was the author of nine New York Times best-selling books, movie producer of *The Shadow Effect*, creator and facilitator of "The Shadow Process" workshop and the founder of *The Ford Institute*. I am honored and privileged to have trained with her and coach people through many of her effective, transformational coaching models. I am grateful for her work which led to my discovery of my own body of work supporting People Pleaser reform.

It was through learning and training with *The Ford Institute* that my spiritual side began to blossom. Before that, I had no faith that my life would work out positively. I was insecure, lacked trust in myself and my capabilities, and was People-Pleasing my way through life. If I hadn't found deeper meaning through my journey, I wouldn't be doing what I am today, and you wouldn't be holding this book.

The first step to making yourself and your life a priority is to find the inspiration and motivation to do so. That must come from a greater knowing that there is support and guidance from a force larger than yourself, whether you call that God, the Divine, the Universe, or Love.

Each day I connect to the joy and peace of knowing there's an unseen, Higher Power that has my back. I know that if I allow it, I can live an extraordinary life. I felt the comfort of this conversation like an infant rocked to sleep by a lullaby. I didn't consciously connect with my spiritual side like I do today, and I was living a toxic life with my faith misplaced by my fear and the belief that life was hard, scary, and unfair.

With my newfound spiritual path, I felt brighter and lighter, although I still felt stuck in many areas of my life, which was evident in my relationships. As much as I love the teachings of Buddhists and some of today's inspirational teachers such as Marianne Williamson, Deepak Chopra, Wayne Dyer, Eckhart Tolle, Mike Dooley, and many others, I needed more clarity. These teachings insist that we're spiritual beings living a human experience and that what we call reality is an illusion. This powerful message brought me comfort, but it didn't help me navigate my day-to-day life and challenges other than having a positive mind-set. I wanted to learn how to live in the "illusion" effectively and be happy within the reality I lived in with my five senses while knowing the unseen was supporting me. Having faith in the unseen is essential, but so is having trust in what's *seen* to live an extraordinary life.

As I coached clients over the years, I began to notice uncanny similarities between my life and the many clients who voiced their disappointment about having done a substantial amount of self-discovery work but remained feeling incomplete and stuck. Almost all of my clients used the words, "I lost myself," when asked what they lost in the outcome of their dysfunctional relationships.

Once I connected People-Pleasing as the reason for my relationship dramas, I began to see that most of the people around me—if not all of the people to some degree or another—were People Pleasers. Many of them didn't know it, and the ones who did couldn't stop it. We were all victims to the myth that doing for others while sacrificing ourselves makes us "good." When you add not believing in a benevolent force that guides and protects you, the picture becomes grim.

"I don't have a spiritual side, and I don't believe I ever will," wrote Donna on a form I asked her to complete.

Not only is Donna a People Pleaser, but she is also codependent in her relationships.

Wikipedia defines codependency as an "excessive emotional or psychological reliance on a partner, typically a partner who requires support due to an illness or addiction."

In relationships, codependency is an emotional and behavioral condition that affects an individual's ability to have a healthy, mutually satisfying relationship.

When we don't have positive experiences in life, or we grow up in either hyper-religious homes or ones without any spiritual guidance, we may question whether or not we're supported as individuals. This questioning makes it easy to blame that which is absent in our lives when we need them most, including parents, spouses, friends, and even God.

Donna's experience reflects this lack since many of her relationships have been dissatisfying and abusive. It's no wonder she suffers from low self-esteem and has a shortage of spiritual belief.

When I attended Debbie Ford's three-day "The Shadow Process" workshop, she asked an unexpected question while leading the participants in an internal visualization exercise. The room was dark. Everyone was instructed to close their eyes and use their breath to imagine floating down inside to access their inner wisdom for answers. There was soft music playing in the background to help everyone relax. She first reminded us to raise our hand if we needed tissues. And then she asked the question that received an astounding reaction from all sixty-seven people in the room. Hands shot up, and the room was filled with the sounds of crying, sobbing, even wailing. The workshop assistants sprang into action and moved at a hurried pace to put tissues in all the raised hands.

Her question: "How young were you when God abandoned you?"

At some point in our lives, no matter who we are, what religion we adhere to or not, we question who we are, where we're going, and whether or not we're loved and supported. If we're People-Pleasing and not bonded to ourselves, not living authentically according to our own needs and desires, we're likely asking the following question frequently because this behavior causes much discomfort with the self: *Is there something out there that has my back?*

Without our connection to ourselves, and lacking faith in a power outside of ourselves, we can fall many times, with each incident diminishing hope as quickly as the time it takes for a bathtub to be drained of water.

People Pleasers abandon themselves early on to juggle the requests of everyone else, so there's no time, energy, or motivation left to address the self effectively. Even when the desire is there, and the effort is attempted, nothing sticks because there's too much space to fill. People-Pleasing leaves you feeling as if you've lost yourself, which you have on many levels.

People-Pleasing isn't the same as pleasing people, because People Pleasers are taught they don't count, they're unimportant, or don't matter. This lesson sets self-abandonment in motion, which means bonding isn't possible. People-Pleasing creates a life that is detached, deceptive, and inauthentic.

The lack of self-bonding and self-care ensures that love, acceptance, and validation must come from the outer world instead of from within the self. People-Pleasing means we eventually push away all that we seek because we're wearing a *giving to get* persona. We feel empty. When we get angry and resentful and blame others for the way we feel, we diminish our power over what we do have control over—ourselves.

Those of us lucky enough to receive positive affirmations from those we cater to, have the opportunity to enjoy the infrequent shots of instant gratification. But there are never enough of those comments to fill up our emptiness. We became obsessed and compelled to do more, more, more.

We do more despite our misgivings in relationships driven mainly by the fear of being alone. We fail to recognize that feeling alone is present in toxic and dysfunctional relationships. It's at the heart of why we struggle. "I feel more alone in this relationship than when I was single!" is a statement frequently said by People Pleasers.

Making yourself your number one priority can only occur once you've made the journey back to you, which means reforming from the destructive behavior you've been engaging in for a lifetime. It means reclaiming your lost self.

The ultimate first step is willingness. You must first be open to not knowing how to move beyond People-Pleasing but have a strong desire to find out. You can't do this without your permission. I'm going to bet that if you've gotten this far in this book, you've acknowledged that you're a People Pleaser. Keep reading to find your way out of this tormented life.

CHAPTER 13

TAKING IT PERSONALLY

Turn your wounds into wisdom.

~ Oprah Winfrey

"Cool," my father would say. "Very Cool. Cold. Ice Cold!"

I would change direction quickly and look elsewhere.

"Warm. Warmer. Hot. Burning hot!" my father would shout.

When I was a little girl, I believed my father was God. He was everything to me. My dad could have easily been mistaken for the young actor James Dean posing in his black leather jacket. The resemblance was uncanny. I loved being around him. Whenever he entered or left a room, I could smell the scent of Old Spice.

The game we often played is still fresh in my mind. My father called it "Hot Potato, Cold Potato."

He'd take a small potato out of the fridge and tell me to close my eyes while he hid it. "Kid," as he fondly called me, was my cue to open my eyes and begin searching high and low. The farther away I was from the potato, the colder it got. The closer I was, the hotter. When I discovered the secret hiding place, I'd hold the potato tightly in my hand, throw up my arms, and giggle.

"Please, Daddy!" I'd say. "Hide it again!"

If I were lucky, we'd play a few times.

Today I think of this game when I meet new people. As much as I believe everyone comes into our lives for a reason, some people are meant to stay, and others are not. It brings me comfort to view the world in this way, because as an avid People Pleaser most of my life, I was always juggling too many potatoes. I needed everyone to like me. I see now how unrealistic this was and how it set me up for a lot of unnecessary disappointment. If there's one lesson that sticks with me now, it's that nothing lasts forever. In the past, I needed to hang onto that belief.

The people I surround myself with now, and the new ones I meet and befriend, I refer to as Hot Potatoes. Everyone is a teacher, and has a place in my life, as I can learn from all of them. I have the choice of who I want to remain in my circle. Hot potatoes are the relationships that bring joy and connection. The Cold Potatoes aren't a joyful match but are important since lessons can be learned from them as well.

As you begin to move away from People-Pleasing, do recognize that you won't like everyone you meet and there will be people who won't like you. I remember I was bothered if others didn't like me, but I remember more acutely feeling uncomfortable when I didn't like others. To minimize this discomfort, I'd rationalize the bad feelings I had and justify keeping people I wasn't fond of around. That was a big mistake. I endured relationships with people I didn't get along with and whom I did not respect.

Because I wasn't bonded with myself and relied heavily on the opinions of my parents and others, I became a chameleon. I molded myself into whatever was needed of me at the time. As time went on though, I felt increasingly uncomfortable with myself. The charade became unbearable, hence the panic attacks I experienced in my early forties.

It takes a toll when we push away our true feelings to not disappoint or to live up to the choices of others. By agreeing, acquiescing, saying it's okay, and trying to convince ourselves that we're doing the best involved for everyone by rationalizing and justifying our actions away, we inadvertently raise our self-loathing bully. When the bully kicks in, it becomes that much harder to stop People-Pleasing. We can no longer help ourselves because of our self-hate. We're left relying on others for validation and approval.

There's a way to stop this behavior. We can turn our lives around by taking everything personally. How many times have you heard the phrase, "Don't take it personally!"? How many times has it rolled off of your tongue when advising others not to feel bad about the circumstances they're sharing with you? We take everything personally whether we admit it or not. Even when we're busy leaving ourselves out as we do things for others, we're doing it for personal gain. Since this is the case, we might as well do it in a way that serves us.

By taking things personally, you'll realize three critical benefits. You'll...

1. Take responsibility for being the common denominator and ever-present witness in *all* your experiences.
2. Stop trying to control everything and start minding your own business and allow others to start minding theirs.
3. Recognize that everything is happening *for* you and not *to* you.

Taking things personally can be empowering!

But, as point number one suggests, you must admit that the way you see the world and the beliefs you hold are yours, and yours alone. What you think, believe, and do attracts those things that show up for you. You have control over a part of your experience. For example, consider your self-image. How you see yourself attracts what you believe you deserve. You attract all your experiences based on how you see yourself, so what you see and take part in is reflected to you from that position. You've been one hundred percent accurate in your perspectives of everything in the past—from *your* vantage point.

Before you put down this book, know that I'm not saying what happens to you is all your fault. Understand, though, that you're not completely blameless, either. The questions you need to ask yourself are:

• How do I change the mental picture of myself to travel to a different vantage point?

- Do I want to move to another place so that I can see things differently?

If you're not experiencing joy and peace in your life, your answer to the last question must be an emphatic, *Yes*!

The second point above suggests that if you're People-Pleasing and using all efforts to obtain the things you need and desire by attending to everyone else but you, then at some deep level you must believe that you can control the outer world. You must also believe at a deep level that what lies in the outside world is the answer to your happiness. If that's your reality, let me assure you it hasn't worked for anyone else so far.

The third point declares that it's time to open your eyes, get the support you need, and try something new to help you reshape your self-image. For a time, you'll have to "fake it until you feel it." Only one or two positive experiences are needed to help you begin creating a new reality.

The Law of Attraction is a universal law that has no exceptions. It states that everything is energy and all energy connects via vibrational frequencies. Because our thoughts and beliefs are also energy, it stands to reason that what we think about, we bring about. (A wealth of information exists on the Law of Attraction; all you have to do is search online. I highly recommend you read up on this subject, because it has a direct impact on your life.)

The experiences you attract, including the most challenging ones, present opportunities for *you* to learn something. Everything in your life is happening for a reason. Nothing happens by chance even if it appears that way. There are no accidents or coincidences other than when and if you choose to see an experience that way. Remember, skepticism is a vantage point. It's been my personal experience as well as some of the clients I've had the privilege to support that the unhappiest people are those who see life as a series of random events and lack the faith that life will work out for them.

Seeing life from a higher vantage point requires moving from your present viewpoint to higher ground. You can imagine you're climbing a large hill or a mountain. Everything looks different from various angles and heights. If you don't like what you're seeing, *move*!

It all begins with changing the way you see you. Once you see yourself in a more favorable light, you'll be lifted to higher ground. Have some faith that there's goodness in your journey, your destination will be joyful, and the life you have lived until now makes sense from your new vantage point. Changing your outlook allows you to travel from vantage points that were once dark and grim to ones that are positive and magical.

Since I have a pretty wild imagination, I've created a scenario to explain the events in my life and how I'm always being supported. I've shared this scenario with my clients and many of them love this perspective and have taken it on for themselves.

Imagine that a special twelve-member Board of Directors has been assigned to you. They meet each week at a specified time in a floating, glass room. On all sides, including the floor and ceiling, only blue sky and scattered clouds are visible. The members sit comfortably around a large, polished mahogany table in this unusual space.

As it is every week, the topic of discussion is *you*, specifically whether or not you're understanding the lessons they're orchestrating on your behalf. When you are applying the lessons, there's little for them to discuss. But when you're not, which happens frequently, they put their heads together to conjure up some scenario that'll throw you flat on your butt to make you pay attention. The proverbial wake-up call. You might feel as if "the rug has been pulled out from underneath you." Regardless of what you feel, the destination is better known as "rock bottom." Your Board doesn't give up until they've pissed you off enough to force you to make a different choice. They care deeply about you and work continuously on your behalf.

When it comes to our relationships with others, all the people we've met and will meet are our teachers and players. They come into our lives to teach us lessons and play out the orchestrated dramas to support us in becoming our greatest self. We're also teachers and players for others.

In the school of life, we need many teachers. The people we meet bring us the lessons we need at the appropriate times when we're ready to learn them. Sometimes we learn the lessons offered to us, and other times we need new teachers to enforce the wisdom we haven't yet received. The reference to players means the same thing. Teachers and players are the people we interact with who bring different circumstances to support our lessons.

This perspective of teachers and players can be comforting when a relationship ends. While it may be hard to let a relationship go, when you frame it as integral to your growth, it becomes easier to understand and accept the relationship had served its purpose.

One relationship that will last forever is the one you have with yourself. Once you focus all your efforts on bonding with yourself and being your loyal anchor, you'll learn to trust your decisions making them clearer and easier to make. You'll also know who's a Hot or Cold Potato and make grounded choices as to whom you keep in your life.

Deciding to take it personally is a choice that will serve you well. You'll see that all of your experiences have a place. Every lesson helps to untie the bow on the gift that is your life. It's your responsibility to support that process.

Nothing is more empowering than relying on yourself and finding peace in your pain.

PART 3

REINVENTING YOU

CHAPTER 14

MAKING THE COMMITMENT TO *STOP*

*When people want to be liked for what they did,
they should stop.*

~ Karl Lagerfeld

"Hold your nose and jump in!" my father shouted to me.

I was only four years old, and my body was small and lanky. I was wearing a red, one-piece swimsuit with a navy-blue anchor in the right corner. I wore a white bathing cap which was secured tightly by a strap underneath my chin.

"Go ahead," he shouted.

I was terrified. It was eighty degrees outside, and my body was shaking. I looked over at my father, got my little fingers in position, squeezed my nostrils together, squinted my eyes tightly, and jumped.

I remember the lake water being very cold. My eyes were closed, and I could sense the blackness underneath. Frightened, I clumsily swam to the surface. Once my head was above the water, I could hear my father applauding and laughing. When I opened my eyes, I saw the overwhelming joy on his face. Confidence flowed through me, and I swam in his direction. When I reached him, he picked me up and hugged me. I wasn't afraid anymore.

When you began this book, you might have been scared, unsure, desperate, and losing hope that life could be better. You now know that as a People Pleaser, your life hasn't been what you expected because of something you learned in childhood. You've paid dearly in your relationships because of it. If you're still unsure whether this book can help you, I invite you to jump in; be brave. The water's fine. I assure you there's a better way to live, and you have the ability and control to make it happen. You don't have to rely on anyone else to stop People-Pleasing. It's solely up to you to turn things around.

Reforming from People-Pleasing first requires your willingness and desire. Without those two qualities, there's no result because there's no process. I hope you can see how the benefits outweigh the costs noted in earlier chapters. I can tell you; it gets harder to change the older you get. You'll have less energy to try to change your behavior, and it might feel futile. It's not. You'll reap the rewards of your investment in big ways. The biggest way will be you reclaiming the self you lost so long ago and start living Your Happy Life Realized.

But first, here are a couple of caveats you need to know.

Once a People Pleaser, always a People Pleaser. I don't call myself a *non*-People Pleaser; I refer to myself as a People Pleaser in Reform (PPIR). Just like a smoker who's quit after many years, the desire to smoke doesn't completely go away, and neither does the residual damage to the lungs. They may have stopped smoking, but there's evidence that they were once a smoker.

In the same way, the many different expressions of People-Pleasing will tug at you now and then, so don't make those desires bad or wrong. As you travel the path of reform, it will become easier for you to make healthy changes.

The confidence you'll gain by making these changes will blend with your present expression to form a humbleness that's authentic and attractive. Your big heart will pay off because you'll be connected and bonded with it, too.

You'll feel discomfort in this process. But if you're radically honest with yourself, you'll admit that you're already uncomfortable and have been for some time. You'll be trading one yucky feeling for another. The big difference is that this new yucky feeling will pass quickly and support the return on investment of your efforts.

Your relationships will also experience ebbs and flows. As your confidence grows, you won't be willing to put up with the behaviors you enable currently, and you'll learn to set effective boundaries so the people who were using you, and there are probably a few, won't be able to anymore. You may even decide to give some people their walking papers.

People come and go in our lives. While we don't have control over other people's thoughts, feelings, actions, or behaviors, we do have control over who remains in our sacred circle. Don't forget: We become who we hang out with.

In a short time, you will be reaping the rewards of being a PPIR. You'll wake up in the morning feeling confident, kinder, peaceful, compassionate, excited, motivated, inspired, rested, and ready to live!

Where you once felt an obligation to do for others, you'll instead feel a sense of longing and a desire to impact and inspire others in different and bigger ways. With your newfound inner respect, your contributions will garner respect from others. Remember, you'll teach people how to treat you by how you treat yourself. In time, you'll become your greatest admirer and enjoy the greatest love of all: self-love.

CHAPTER 15

THE PATH TO SELF-FORGIVENESS

Forgiveness is the key to happiness.

~ A Course in Miracles

"You don't sound angry to me."

I've said this countless times to clients. They share outrageous stories that are worthy of a Lifetime movie. I sit stunned as they describe events with a monotone voice and an obvious lack of emotion. I'm getting angry as I listen; why aren't they?

"Why don't you sound angry?" I ask.

Very often they answer that they're pissed, but there's no indication in their voice and no reaction around what they're sharing. Meanwhile, I feel like throwing things across the room on their behalf.

Most of the clients I support minimize what they've lived through. Their stories of abuse are hard to believe, and they resist owning that they were victimized by denying it or glossing over the circumstances.

My expertise as a life coach is supporting people in deep healing by reinterpreting their journeys in ways that empower them. The intention is to get them out of their victim story; however, to move powerfully into the victor story, they must acknowledge the depth of their victimization and how it changed them.

You must own your truth first because your past lives within you. It must be fully dealt with and healed. Otherwise, if you don't make peace with it, your past will fester within the folds of your psyche and blindside you at the most inopportune times causing you to miss opportunities that come your way.

Owning your victim story means you can no longer minimize, justify, or rationalize other people's bad behavior. If you're unwilling to own your story, you'll hold onto the resentment and continue to struggle. Reveal what happened, own that you were victimized, and give your emotions room to be expressed. There is no shame in being emotional; anger, sadness, frustration, and disgust are legitimate feelings. You may find that writing your story is an effective way to recall your experiences. Don't stop writing when your emotions flare, keep going. Their presence means you're bringing up crucial and painful pieces.

A big step toward owning your story is recognizing that your memory of your experience is one hundred percent accurate for you. Don't let others influence your perspective and stay true to yours. You can't move to different vantage points and see things differently if you doubt the way you see things or continue to question yourself. It's time to put self-doubt to bed and start trusting yourself.

You'll begin to heal in magical ways after you stop minimizing what happened to you. You can choose to use your story to serve you instead of sabotage you. When you own your victim story, it's fully yours to forgive. You become the victor, no longer living at the mercy of another's abuse.

If you're ready to cultivate the inspiration and motivation to fuel yourself to keep moving forward in life, your positive acknowledgment is crucial. For all the years you've beat yourself up, it's now time to thank and recognize yourself and all your efforts toward making better choices to live a valued life. Positive acknowledgment recognizes a job well-done and allows you to give yourself long overdue credit.

Acknowledgment is praising yourself for all that you do and being thankful for your accomplishments and your tenacity to keep moving forward even when doing so feels awful. Acknowledgment provides self-validation and enables you to see yourself in a positive light. Finally, positive acknowledgment works diligently in your subconscious to change your negative self-image into a positive one that makes you grateful and honored to be *you*.

Self-forgiveness is a critical part of acknowledgment. Self-forgiveness is necessary because it addresses all the things in your life that you feel bad about, that remain unresolved, and that you resist bringing to closure. Self-forgiveness allows you to grieve and process your losses while gaining the lessons.

Many People Pleasers are angry at themselves for bringing about the compromises and violations in their lives. They blame themselves as well as others for the transgressions that have caused them pain.

Anger at the self makes sense when you consider how often you put aside your needs and wants for those of others. But self-forgiveness can be difficult for People Pleasers. Consider this: Would you forgive someone who has lied, offended, betrayed, and broken promises to you repeatedly? Your answer is most likely an emphatic *no*! But if you examine the relationship you have with yourself, you'll see the repeat offender. You consistently disregard yourself even though you might say, "This is the last time" when you're asked to do for others. It usually *is* the last time, until you do it again. Trust is a crucial component of forgiveness. It's virtually impossible to forgive with any lasting effect without it. So, once you forgive yourself, you *must stop* the People-Pleasing behavior that has you out of integrity with yourself. Otherwise, nothing will change, and you'll have betrayed yourself . . . again.

That's why self-forgiveness is so important to your People-Pleasing reform. You can't effectively go into your future burdened by your past transgressions. Even though the past will be part of your future, you need to forgive yourself for not taking better care to protect yourself from painful things. The key to forgiveness is understanding that you behaved based on how you saw yourself then and that you continued to make bad choices because you lacked confidence or self-worth and sabotaged yourself instead. It's time to cut yourself some slack and recognize that your insecurities got the best of you.

Love goes along with forgiveness. In an earlier chapter, I expressed my dislike of unconditional love as it relates to you plus others. As with many things in life, there's a caveat to unconditional love. I believe you must love yourself unconditionally. It's important to forgive your transgressions and discover the love you have for yourself despite what you've done in the past.

Self-forgiveness is tremendously powerful because it allows you to love yourself while not excusing your bad behavior. It's hard to become a better person if you don't like yourself or keep rehashing your past mistakes.

My client, Cecilia, is an example of a woman who was unwilling to move past the life she feels she screwed up.

"Noooooooo!" Cecilia cried out during a self-forgiveness session when asked to forgive the parts of herself that she hated.

Cecilia is in her early fifties, has never married or had children, and harshly judges herself as a loser and a spinster. She thinks she's ugly and has a long list of what's wrong with her. I felt a strong resistance on her part to find compassion and kindness for the little girl part of her that was severely wounded.

Cecilia was a precocious, active child. Her mother, impatient and intolerant, would lock her in a closet. Cecilia, alone in the dark, would spend her time screaming. Even though she had tremendous resentment toward her mother for abusing her as a child, she hated herself more for being what she called, "an unwanted, bad little girl."

Cecilia has many ailments including sleep apnea. She's convinced she has deep learning disabilities and does little to help herself emotionally. Our coaching work together was a new experience for her, and even though she made some strides, I could feel her resistance to forgiving herself.

Cecilia is a fervent People Pleaser. She offers her assistance everywhere and reminds me of a juggler with too many balls. She also has a big heart and doesn't see how interesting and fun she is to be around when her insecurities aren't getting the best of her. I hope someday she sees how incredibly special she is.

My client, Ellen, healed leaps and bounds because of her willingness to forgive herself for staying in her emotionally and physically abusive marriage for years after her pastor and family convinced her divorce was not an option.

Ellen cried during many of our sessions, a sure sign of release and healing. When it came time to forgive herself, she was ready, willing, and able to show compassion and love to all the parts of herself she disliked. She was also able to understand how she'd compromised and violated herself in this marriage because she felt incapable of handling the consequences of going against her family and her church.

Despite what others wanted for Ellen, she stood up for herself and her children's safety and sought a divorce. As she continued to forgive herself, she was able to handle the challenges that came her way almost effortlessly.

Today, Ellen has a good relationship with her ex, and they co-parent their children. Everyone is happy. She's also involved in a new, loving relationship with a great man and is furthering her career as a businesswoman.

In my own life, I continue to forgive myself for getting into unhealthy relationships, leaving them, and returning to them. I now understand that then I strongly believed I could change people and had faith the relationship would get better. I imagined a rosy-colored picture and glossed over the toxicity I was living in.

Whereas I once felt frustrated, foolish, and stupid, I now know that I didn't love myself back then and attracted what I believed I deserved. It took time, dedication, and commitment to continue forgiving myself. I'll continue this process as long as I'm breathing.

To forgive deeply, I've developed a practice to support myself and my clients. I invite you to give it a try.

Self-Forgiveness Recommended Practice

Make two lists on a piece of paper. Label the first list *All The Things I Dislike About Myself.* Label the second list *All The Bad Choices I Made In My Life.* You can make each list as long as you wish but write at least ten to twenty items on each. My lists are below.

All the Qualities I Dislike About Myself:

I'm judgmental.

I'm impatient.

I'm critical and controlling.

I'm insecure.

I'm weak.

I'm fearful.

I hide from others.

I'm scared to speak up.

I let others walk all over me.

I never finish anything.

I beat myself up a lot.

I'm self-abusive.

I never let myself off the hook.

I take responsibility for other's actions.

I forgive others who don't apologize or respect me.

I don't set boundaries.

All the Bad Choices I Made in My Life

Did things I didn't want to do; i.e., with men, in jobs, for my parents.

Allowed people to get away with treating me badly.

Did not demand respect.

Got into drugs and unhealthy behaviors that were dangerous.

Hung out with the wrong crowd.

Didn't take my education seriously.

Didn't work hard when I needed to.

Never had the children I always wanted.

Was mean and abusive to other people because of how I felt.

Made other people responsible for my feelings.

Believed people's pleas and promises when I knew better.

Gave everyone the benefit of the doubt without knowing them.

Married people I knew were wrong for me.

Blamed my parents for everything.

Played myself down so others could shine and be happy.

Remained a victim for decades and held myself back.

Next, write a *letter of apology* to your innocent, wounded inner child to let him, or her know what happened in your life wasn't their fault. If you have a picture of yourself as a child, find it and put it next to you as you write. In this letter, let your inner child know that all these violations were done at a time when you were making bad decisions due to not feeling worthy and apologize profusely to them. Acknowledge the suffering you both endured and commit to making it up to the both of you.

Letter of Apology

My dear little Evie,
Words can't express all the pain and sorrow I feel for all that I brought your way.

I can't imagine how betrayed you felt and how afraid you must have been when you felt trapped as a result of all the bad choices I made.

I'm so sorry for all the times I've put you in harm's way.

There are no words to sum up the sadness and guilt I feel to have treated you so unfairly for nothing that was ever your fault.

You're a true angel to have given me so many opportunities to prove my love for you and to do things differently even though many times I was just one disappointment after another.

Evie, if you'll give me this chance, and I pray to God with all of my might that you will, I promise to make you the *Number One Love of My Life* and treat you like the sacred, beautiful soul that you are.

You're my inspiration and greatest purpose. I commit to know you fully and honor you every day for the rest of my life. I vow never to promise anything I can't keep and start now by taking the vow to never again compromise and violate you by putting you in situations that by my choice are harmful, disrespectful, or humiliating.

I promise you I'll stop People-Pleasing and let go of the judgments of others that I ultimately took out on you until you were exhausted, sad, and hopeless.

I look forward to a life of peace, joy, and happiness. And from now on, you call all the shots! I won't make any choices without running them by you first.

My undying love,

Eve

Making your lists and writing your letter can generate some raw emotions. Allow them to come. Have a good cry, beat a pillow for five minutes, lock yourself in your car and scream, or close your eyes and find some much-needed peace and tranquility.

I hope you recognize that your letter, while written to your inner child, is written to you from you, and in it, you made some serious promises. This letter gives you full immunity for all your transgressions and allows you to begin anew by taking full responsibility for your present and future actions. Please take this work seriously because, if you go back on your word, your inner child won't trust you and you won't trust yourself. Staying in integrity must be your number one choice and priority. After all, you've done some hard work, and you want your powerful results to last.

After forgiving yourself, you must stay true to the promises you made. Your inner child has been burned for decades by your actions. That child needs ample consistency and commitment to warm up to you and trust you again. Your inner child wants to forgive you, but you must be willing to *earn* that forgiveness and live with integrity.

Even though you're focusing on you, you'll also want to acknowledge that you must forgive others, too. Recognizing that you were who you were at the time, they were who they were at that time, too. It's likely you hooked up with people who didn't like themselves either; the perfect mix for a toxic relationship. Forgiving others isn't about condoning or relieving them of responsibility or saying everything that happened is acceptable. To move beyond the ways you've attracted pain into your life, release any resentments toward others and cherish the peace that letting go can bring.

You can support this process by writing two lists and a letter of apology as you did above. Only this time, you'll make a list of the qualities you disliked in the other person and a list of their transgressions that resulted due to the way they treated you. Next, having the faith that they, like you, didn't like themselves, you'll imagine and then write a letter of apology to you from them. In it will be all the things you need to hear. Even though you're writing the letter, the act of giving a voice to their apology does positively affect and support you to release the resentment you have toward the other person.

I worked deeply with forgiveness during one of my separations from my husband, Matt. It felt so loving. I entered a vibration I'd never felt before. But instead of using the feeling of being enveloped in love to move on, I mistook the feeling as a chance for reconciliation.

We did reconcile, but it ultimately fell apart again because forgiveness doesn't change a relationship; forgiveness gives closure. Each time I went back into the marriage, I violated myself. Each time I left, I had to work on forgiving myself all over again.

Had I left things alone and basked in my new positive feelings of forgiveness, learned my lessons, and continued counting my prayers, I'd have saved myself a lot of grief. Forgiveness can feel incredibly loving, but it doesn't—and—shouldn't wipe the slate clean. I'm not suggesting we should hold on to resentment. I'm suggesting that bad *past* behavior will become bad *present* behavior whether we're compassionate or not.

Forgiving others is important, but in People Pleaser reform, the focus should remain on you. As you navigate the self-forgiveness process, thus bringing more compassion for yourself into your life, you'll also be facilitating your forgiveness of others.

The most effective way to forgive yourself is to stop interacting with the people involved *if you have an option to do so*. When it comes to families, this isn't always possible, although you may want to keep your distance from family members who are toxic or negatively affect you. But when a friend, girlfriend/boyfriend, or significant other has betrayed you, the best way to powerfully solidify your self-forgiveness is by ending that relationship. You'll eliminate the constant reminder of the wrongs you've been subjected to. More important, you'll be making the profound statement of "I forgive you, and I will give to you no more." I call this statement *No-Moregiveness*.

I forgive you, and I give to you no more.

Speaking from personal experience, this is a sure way to get someone out of your life and out of your mind while keeping your integrity in check. And, it's the most loving choice all around because giving to someone who's offended or betrayed you is sure to make you feel like a fool. Once you declare *No-Moregiveness*, you're declaring to others and the world, "I forgive you, and I'm complete with you. You deserve no more from me, and I give you no more." Trust me; it's a big-time confidence booster.

When you feel complete with the process, send light and love to everyone involved. Close your eyes, picture these people in your mind, and say "Goodbye, thanks for the lessons!" Then wish that all the lessons will support your and their growth.

If you're resisting sending good wishes to those who've hurt you, it's okay. You don't have to like them. However, don't dwell or give any time or attention to your inability to forgive because it will eat away at you and kill your joy. The best revenge is moving forward and creating a great life for yourself.

I forgive Matt, and I also don't like him. I nicknamed him, "Nice guy, not so nice." Still, I wish him well. Truly, I don't think of him at all anymore, unless I'm using him as an example in coaching or writing.

If you're wondering what to do with the people who will remain in your life, I've come up with a helpful way to manage them while keeping your expectations in check. Forgive and read on.

CHAPTER 16

COMPARTMENTALIZING THE PEOPLE IN YOUR LIFE

Some people believe holding on and hanging
in there are signs of great strength.
However, there are times when it takes much
to know when it's time to let go and then to do it.

~ Ann Landers

No one is perfect. No relationship is perfect, but the lesson always is.

When I deleted the email that I thought was a promotional advertisement, I didn't realize it was my birthday gift from Allison.

"Did you get the gift?" Allison asked.

"What gift?"

"I'll resend it," she said. "Look out for it. It's from Sephora."

It didn't make sense to me, that after all these years of lavishing each other with extra special gifts, extravagant lunches, and over-the-top surprises, that I was receiving a birthday gift via email whose value had me adding money to buy an eye pencil and lipstick.

Don't get me wrong; getting this sort of gift from a friend is generous. Coming from Allison, it was a huge insult.

Allison was like a sister to me. There was a time I wondered if you could legally adopt a sister, and how Allison would be my pick if you could. She was very special to me, and I considered her my best friend.

I had questioned her loyalty in the past, like when I was going through a divorce and asked her to cut ties with my soon-to-be-ex, and she told me she had to think about it. Despite that, I moved on believing we were good friends. Later, when I discovered she remained in contact with him through Facebook and lied about it, I decided to let that go too, even though it bothered me. I was building a resentment list, but I wasn't aware of it yet.

When I look back, I see that our relationship was lopsided. I remember the ten-plus nights that Allison and her husband Tim stayed at my home. I slept on the couch so Tim, who has a bad back, could sleep comfortably in a bed. I acted like I didn't mind when their adorable dog peed on my carpet. I cooked for them, entertained them, and was supportive of them when they relocated to a new state, and again when they moved back. I bestowed on them added attention, love, and generosity. There were also some other gestures I made on their behalf. These memories now had me scratching my head in confusion. There was a deeper message for me, and I was starting to feel uncomfortable.

I wondered if she and Tim were in financial straits. That notion was quickly dispelled as I looked at the photos she shared on Facebook of extravagant outings to expensive restaurants and shows in New York. I was glad she wasn't in trouble, but the "something" nagging at me wouldn't go away. When I thought long and hard about it, I came to the hurtful conclusion that I was being used.

The epiphany hit me hard. I could see the People Pleaser I was and how that led me to believe I needed to overdo for others to be liked. This realization made me sad, and it made me mad at them and myself. I decided it was time to end my relationship with Allison.

I owe this eye-opening experience to my relationship with Allison because had this relationship not been a close one, I would have missed the lesson. An insulting birthday gift turned out to be the present of the century. I could see that Allison and I were great teachers for each other. My next step influenced our growth and evolution. It was a step I needed to take for me.

I admired Allison as a woman with enormous strength. Her survival to rise above some difficult life circumstances was inspiring. I could see her potential as a person. I had to put those thoughts aside for it was time to stand up for me, and I knew I'd lose her friendship in the process. Speaking out was a bold move I had to take. Otherwise, the lessons wouldn't stick for either of us.

Cowardly as it may be, I chose to send a letter to Allison by snail mail. It was a heartfelt letter but a Dear John Letter nonetheless. I was ending our friendship. I wrote how I thought she was a great woman and that I would cherish the memories we shared. I also let her know that I was deeply hurt, thought her gift was insulting, and that her selection of it spoke volumes to me.

I left out the disappointment around the many plans she'd canceled and the disconnection I felt in our relationship as a result of her not being available. I also left out the part about how I felt her disloyalty as a friend and that I was feeling used by her and Tim.

"I will not spend time with people who don't respect, honor or appreciate my kindness," I wrote. I just wanted to move on.

When I received a jaw-dropping litany of insults about me via text, I responded immediately.

"Well now, your gift makes sense," I wrote back. *"Please do not contact me again."*

"As you wish," she replied.

And so, my healing began.

Whenever you hear harsh and hurtful judgments from someone whom you've extended your kindness and generosity to, it's usually for one of two reasons. One is that they know they screwed up and are deflecting it by defending themselves and not owning responsibility. The other is that they're deeply hurt and too self-absorbed to care that you got hurt in the process. When you're a People Pleaser, others can act in ways that make you think you've gone crazy, and yet you'll take full responsibility for everything.

Now, it was up to me to stick to my decision to cut Allison out of my life.

As I believe all relationships are cocreated, I hardly wash my hands of any fault and know I enabled the relationship to go on as it did. There were things I did that contributed to the demise of this relationship. In the bigger picture, where everything happens for a reason, and we have players and teachers that come and go in our lives, the losses and lessons must come and go, too.

Over the next year, Allison sent me a couple of emails. In one, she apologized for her behavior and said she was going through a lot at the time. She declared that she loves me unconditionally, which had a hidden meaning for me. She again deflected her responsibility and inferred that I did something wrong and that she loves me despite that. She never once mentioned she was sorry that I felt hurt.

When people apologize and defend themselves simultaneously, it's a relationship red flag. They're deflecting responsibility for their actions and blaming you. Recognizing this behavior is important information because you want to choose your confrontations with people carefully. Discussions with people who don't take responsibility can be hazardous to People Pleasers because they'll believe what they're being told. People Pleasers are easily manipulated into allowing others to walk all over them once again.

I responded to Allison's email graciously, but I had no intention of reconnecting with her. I didn't hear back. This relationship is a good example of the No-Moregiveness concept I discussed in the last chapter. I set a boundary on my behalf and refused to give any more to someone I chose to forgive and move on from. I don't deny that my letter to Allison hurt her feelings. We all hurt others at times as they hurt us. Sometimes we're just protecting ourselves in the process. It's a part of life.

At this juncture in my journey, it was essential for me to evaluate the people I kept close carefully. I encourage you to proceed with caution and consider whom you surround yourself with.

The bigger the loss, the greater the lessons. I like to call them *Lossons*.

Lossons are the potent wake-up calls that knock us to our knees and then invite us to stand up stronger than before. Without holding ourselves and others accountable, the lessons can't be integrated within us so that we live our lives from a higher vantage point. Without loss, the lesson doesn't stick.

The questions below are designed to help you carefully decide who belongs in your life and in what respect.

- *Are there people in your life who treat you in ways that disappoint, confuse, or offend you?*
- *Are you overly doing for others and experiencing little if no reciprocity from them?*
- *Are you staying in relationships that don't feel good?*
- *Are you afraid to confront others or ask for what you want and need?*
- *Are there inconsistencies in the way others treat you?*

The people that come into our lives appear for a reason. They help us to learn, grow, and become the best people we can be.

Cutting Allison out of my life was the most loving thing I could do for myself and her. Had I chosen otherwise, I would have resented her, been phony and standoffish, and harshly judgmental, all negative energy. That's not a kind choice for anyone.

I can still send love and light to Allison and wish her much joy in her life, even though we're no longer in a relationship. Because I have forgiven her and chosen to no longer give to her, I'm free from any resentments, grudges, or negative judgments. In my heart, I believe this experience has supported her, too. In my imagination, I see her thriving in life and relationships.

To further illustrate what I mean by Lossons, consider the Bruno Mars song, "When I Was Your Man." In it, Mars sings about the regret he has for not giving his woman what she needs. In the process, he lost her to another man. I believe that if this experience hadn't happened as it did, he wouldn't have learned that there are consequences in how we nurture our relationships and that we can lose the people we love. If he takes this lesson of loss to heart, he'll be a greater man and partner.

In the Spring, I attended Tonya and Jane's special day. They celebrated together since their birthdays were one week apart. They selected a pricey restaurant in which to celebrate, expecting their friends to pick up the tab. They both accepted gifts with glee and thanked everyone profusely for making the experience festive and fun. We all had a great time.

The next day, I received a phone call from Tonya. She asked if I could give some money back to Cindy, one of the party-goers, as she was financially strapped and hadn't expected to pitch in for Tonya and Jane's meals, too. I was stunned that Tonya and Jane hadn't even considered giving money to Cindy for their meals. I didn't oblige this request.

When my birthday came around at the end of October, neither Tonya nor Jane acknowledged it with even a phone call, card, gift, or text. It was the third year I was overlooked, and I was angry. So, I sent a text to them both: "Please cancel our plans. Unless I run into you, I won't be seeing you again."

I realized my self-image needed a checkup because I was continuing to attract experiences that made me feel disrespected and rejected. By sending my text, I was saying, *"no and no more."*

Tonya wrote back, "I'm so sorry, dear. Facebook didn't remind me."

Her response further infuriated me, but it also validated that I was making the right choice by walking away.

"Can you forgive me?" Jane replied.

And with that, I let them both know that yes, I did forgive them. I added that I hoped Tonya and Jane would use this experience to be more diligent in the future about honoring their friends and not forget the friends they care about. I also let them know that this experience was a gift to me as well because it caused me to raise my standards about the friends I keep. They no longer qualified.

People can use or take advantage of you only if you allow them to. When Tonya and Jane forgot my birthday again, I paused to question my relationship with them. I examined my behavior and asked myself why I allowed these disappointments to recur without establishing any boundaries or consequences. I knew that I was the one attracting these people into my life, but, until I was forgotten again, I couldn't see how I enabled my experiences to be disappointing. Now I could see it clearly, and it was time for me to take responsibility for my part in it. Even though my reaction was directed toward them, I was angry with myself. Tonya and Jane were who they had always been since I met them: Takers. Their behavior hadn't changed—I changed and was no longer willing to put up with it. They probably felt blindsided by my harsh reaction and thought I'd overreacted. I'd have to agree, but my birthday oversight was just the last straw of many. I was done.

My life became interesting and fascinating as I committed to choosing and losing the people in my life. My confidence soared. My relationships deepened; my connections were stronger. I was delighted and proud of myself.

I also attracted new people whom I admired, and I was giving more to them in a healthy, authentic way because I was giving mostly to me.

Instead of feeling the need to do so much for others to garner their praise, I understood our friendship wasn't contingent on how they felt about me. I did special things for others to honor them because I liked them, not because I was *giving to get*. I was sharing and rejoicing in my ability to contribute to others in positive ways.

Where People-Pleasing is all about getting others to like us, self-love is about filling ourselves up so that we can give and receive love with and from others. That's why it's essential for your self-image to be positive and inspiring, and for you to understand that the people you spend your time with either contribute or take away from how you view yourself.

As much as your self-image attracts the way others treat you, the way people interact with you affects the way you see yourself. One feeds the other. That's why you must set boundaries and make better choices once you're aware that your self-worth is low.

But know that it's not possible to connect with everyone, and we're not meant to. You won't like everyone you meet, and some people won't like you either. Relationships start to make more sense when you accept this fact. It's helpful to see your current and potential relationships for what they are or could be so that your expectations are in check. Having your eyes wide open at the start of every relationship will help prevent an unnecessary disappointment by not reading the relationship accurately.

If you consider my story with Allison, I believe I had high expectations for the relationship and felt more strongly about it than she did. If I'd seen things in a different light, I might not have been as hurt throughout our friendship. Unwittingly, Allison also reinforced a belief I held about myself that I hadn't discovered yet: I wasn't interesting or special. My self-image was selecting my friends. If someone isn't nice to you, it's because you're not thinking nice things about yourself.

When I chose friends, everyone was fair game. I gave everyone the benefit of the doubt even when I didn't have any information about them. I didn't give myself the opportunity to get to know people fully or learn what they were about before entering into a relationship with them. Sometimes the strongest bond I felt was with people who didn't reciprocate. As a People Pleaser, this led me to try harder to be liked. I also avoided acting out any negative feelings such as being angry, mean, selfish, or jealous. I prided myself on my control and my easygoing demeanor. I was only deceiving myself. In truth, I was afraid to express my feelings, set boundaries, or demand respect because I didn't want to hurt the other person.

When the seemingly inevitable rejection occurred, it left me in emotional pain, especially if I'd "overlooked" previous betrayals. Once they were gone, all I had left were my swirling thoughts, which distracted me and caused me to relive the pain repeatedly. It was distressing, and something had to change.

I developed a practice to evaluate the people in my life according to what they mean to me at any given time. Relationship expectations can change, and when I didn't change the relationship to match my expectations, it became uncomfortable. I developed the exercises to give some structure to support my confidence, give me clarity, and, when necessary, provide closure. I've found it also supports my ability to release resentments and grudges more quickly because it prompts me to take immediate action. The best part is I can do this myself. I have full control and don't need anyone else to complete it.

I hope you find the Compartmentalizing Your People practice as helpful as I have. You're free to use the categories I've defined or create your own.

Compartmentalizing Your People

Using this exercise will help you gain clarity about the people in your life and decide whether to demote or promote them or to move them out of your life completely.

If you find this exercise harsh, it could be because you don't fully own your negative feelings. Owning your feelings is essential to placing people in the appropriate compartment. For this exercise to be effective, you must allow yourself to feel what's there. No one needs to know what you're doing, and it's not meant to hurt others. Instead, this exercise is designed to be loving to everyone involved by acknowledging your true feelings and protecting yourself from unnecessary disappointment. You take care of you. Let others take care of themselves.

Extra Special VIP

These are the people who are dear to your heart and whom you love the most. It can be anyone from family members to friends to coworkers. If you have a couple to a handful of these people on this list, you're blessed! These are the people you can count on. You feel comfortable asking for help and expect them to be reliable, loyal, and loving.

You have high expectations for this group because they're your greatest support network. You fully trust them and believe in their sincerity and intentions, and they feel the same about you. You'd go out on a limb for them and expect them to do the same for you. This group represents your biggest personal investment, be it your time, money, or heart. Expectations are the highest here. One or more of these people are likely listed as an emergency contact should anything happen to you.

My list includes me, my cousin, and my sister. I care for myself in new, profound ways and completely rely on myself to be responsible for me. I consider myself my greatest support, which is why I'm number one on my list. My cousin and my sister fit most of the criteria in this group. My cousin has been in my life more closely in the last few years. I trust her and believe she has my best interests at heart. My sister supports me in many ways, and I'm emotionally connected to her as my twin.

I would have placed Allison here if we were still friends. Then, as I experienced inconsistencies in our relationship, I could've demoted her. She may have remained in my life in a different respect. Either way, I would have had different expectations because I would've seen her for who she is and interacted with her on a different level.

If there's big betrayal in this category, you must carefully consider whether to release this person from your life or demote them, provided they aren't family. If you have the flexibility to cut them out of your life, doing so is more effective because you won't be reminded of their betrayal every time you see them. Dealing with family members can be tricky, but you need to take measures to protect yourself when one or more family members are toxic. You can still love people while keeping your distance and limiting your time.

Forgiveness is essential in all demotions or releases, so make sure you do the exercises in the last chapter on self-forgiveness.

Familial Relationships

It's not unusual for disharmony and dysfunction to occur with family members. Some family members will fall into the Extra Special VIP compartment and others won't. Don't feel obligated to place family members in any particular category that doesn't feel comfortable. You can choose to love your family as closely or as distantly as feels right to you. No one has to know your true feelings but you.

Before my father passed away, I would have placed him in this category. I loved him very much, but he was toxic to be around, and he affected me emotionally to the point where it took days to recover. He was verbally and emotionally abusive, and I was no longer going to subject myself to his torture. He also refused to help me with some hardships, so I no longer went to him for support because I didn't feel he'd comply. Taking all these things into account, I chose to love him from a distance. I called him every week to talk about the weather and his golf game. In time, I developed forgiveness and compassion for him.

After he died suddenly at the age of eighty-eight, my forgiveness deepened. I was able to remember some really good times we shared. I live in honor of him today, and I keep a photo of him on the end table in my living room. Every morning and night, I kiss the photo and tell him I love him. I arrived at this compassionate place by honoring my true feelings, which is essential to have and keep healthy relationships in your life.

Inspiring Impact Circle of Friends

These are the people to whom you look to for inspiration and growth. You can talk to them, confide in them, and feel trust and comfort that they have your back and are cheering you on. You enjoy their company and the time you spend with them. You're like-minded, and the sky's the limit with how these relationships can grow. These people represent who you aspire to be. You value these people and their opinions highly. If you have one to three people in this group, you're fortunate. You're willing to invest your time and energy to those in this compartment. But a financial or personal heart-centered investment isn't necessary. Once you have a personal investment with someone in this group, you can consider promoting this person to the Extra Special VIP compartment above.

Expectations in this compartment include respect, consideration, and loving compassion. Big favors or requests may arise, but don't blindly go along. Consider them carefully.

I have a handful of friends on this list and feel blessed to have them in my life. My relationship with these friends has the potential to go into the Extra Special VIP compartment at any time.

Fair Weather Friends

Most people you know will fall into this group. These are the people you know in passing, at work, in all areas of life. You like them, regard them well, and may even socialize with them from time to time. You enjoy each other's company, but a superficiality pervades your relationship. Stronger relationships can develop with people in this compartment and often do since many unions start this way. These people come and go depending on where you live, where you're working, and the social circle you hang out with. Sometimes these connections end because the circumstances that supported them wither away. There's no real personal investment here other than the time spent getting to know them or enjoying their company on a no-risk basis.

Expectations are at a bare minimum here. Asking for help with a project at work, offering to help others out who need minimal support, or listening to a friend vent about her day is what's covered here. The investment on your part is little to none. The name of this compartment pretty much sums it up.

Acquaintances

Acquaintances are people whom you recognize but don't know on any real level. There's potential for these relationships to grow, since people we become deeply connected to start as strangers.

Expectations, if any, should be extremely low to none until you know more about these people and promote them to other compartments. Don't give anyone the benefit of the doubt. Trust is earned.

Walking Papers

This compartment is reserved for those people who were once in any of the above categories but whom you no longer choose to have in your life. As the name suggests, you can imagine handing them walking papers or signing a breach of contract agreement that states you'll no longer be participating in their life. Again, this is for you to find resolution and closure with the people who have offended and hurt you. It's more loving to release people than to keep them around and be angry with them. You can enter a clause in your imaginary walking papers that states this is for the betterment of their lives, too.

While this has been all about you and your needs, it's just as important to respect another person's need for space and time to process the pain in their life. If doing so means they no longer want a connection with you, respect it, and wish them well. Release any grievances you may have so your mind is clear.

Have fun with this practice and remember, no one needs to know. The exercise is for you. It's not necessary to share this with others as it could potentially be hurtful. You'll find that your interactions with people will become more natural, your expectations more realistic, and your effort more appropriate.

CHAPTER 17

FINDING YOUR COMFORT ZONE

The worst loneliness is to not be comfortable with yourself.

~ Mark Twain

"This is hard for me to ask, but could you lend me three thousand dollars?"

A few years ago, I met a guy named Jack through an organization in which we were both members.

Our group met every week, and before long, Jack and I struck up some interesting conversations. He shared stories of his family with me, showed me photos of his children, and I thought he was a nice guy.

The week before Christmas, I noticed Jack wasn't his cheery self. I asked if everything was okay. He shared with me that he was struggling financially and didn't know if he could pay his mortgage that month. I did what I could to comfort him by assuring him things would work out.

When Jack phoned the next day asking for money, I got that gnawing feeling in the pit of my stomach I often get when I'm out of my comfort zone. I hesitated and then said "I can't spare that much, but I'm happy to lend you five hundred dollars. Maybe you could raise the rest from other people."

I usually ask myself when lending money if I can afford to lose it because I don't always get my money back. That year, lending money was a stretch. I calculated what I could do without that month. After all, I had presents to buy and bills to pay, too. I didn't want to end up feeling strapped myself. As uncomfortable as I felt lending the money, I felt more angst not helping Jack.

We met at a local department store. It was busy with last-minute shoppers scurrying around to find the right gifts and check off the names on their Christmas lists. Tinsel was everywhere, "Silent Night" was playing, and there was a long line at the gift-wrapping desk.

I stood at our designated meeting spot in the shoe department and spotted Jack. I gave him the cash, and he promised to pay me back quickly. We hugged and wished each other Happy Holidays.

Two weeks later, Jack resigned from our group. He had landed the job he was waiting for and would no longer have time to come to meetings. I was happy for him.

When two months passed, I became annoyed that Jack hadn't contacted me to repay my loan. After all, he was employed at a new job, and things were looking up. This behavior surprised me. He struck me as a decent, honest, reliable person. I was becoming angry with him and myself.

After months of texting and emailing Jack, getting responses that promised one thing or another with no resolution, I sent a text that got his attention. It was now six months since our transaction.

"If I don't get my money back by the middle of this week, I will take stronger measures, and you won't be happy."

His response came immediately.

"I can meet you on Wednesday. Tell me where and when."

At first, I was thinking of a meeting place that would be mutually convenient for both of us and then assured myself I no longer needed to be considerate. I chose a destination around the corner from where I lived.

When Jack walked into the coffee shop, he looked nervous and uncomfortable.

He handed me an envelope which I accepted.

"I guess you need the money more than I do?" he said. He had a sad, desperate look on his face.

And that's when I felt it. The jab in my stomach that made me want to fall into a hole and disappear. There was a mixture of both anger and guilt. I felt bad taking the money from Jack. Isn't that a hoot? I had the urge to give it back to him and tell him he could pay me later.

While my heartstrings were being played, my stomach was turning in knots. I didn't sway and told Jack how disappointed I was with him.

"I would never treat my friends badly," he insisted.

"You already did," I stated. "I'm incredibly surprised you acted the way you did. Maybe it's time to learn the lesson of not taking advantage of people's kindness," I added.

As a People Pleaser, I had difficulty standing up for myself all of my life, easily getting sucked into abandoning my own needs and desires even if I knew deep down that people were using me. It's why I felt like a fool much of the time. I'd had enough. I was committed to finding ways to be loving to myself while letting others know where I stood. My experience with Jack was a huge lesson; lending money was just a small part of it. As much as I wanted to help Jack, it wasn't my responsibility. I needed to learn that I must put my life first even if that means having to say no to someone in need.

People Pleasers have a hard time accepting the darker side of humanity. They can't see their deception with their People-Pleasing behavior and dread seeming to be negative. They also have big hearts. Learning to put themselves first will avoid the potential of being hurt by wanting to help. That's why a big step in People Pleaser reform is finding their comfort zone and discovering what's acceptable or not to them. It's a lesson in integrity 101.

I wondered what would've happened if Jack hadn't paid me back. I know that when I was People-Pleasing, I would've been angry but rationalized or justified it away. I would've considered whether asking for the money back was selfish and then decided that I should be kind and extend it as a gift. Even though I had a right to confront Jack, I concluded I wouldn't have been so reactive if I hadn't been angry about doing something that I didn't want to do in the first place.

The big lesson out of my experience with Jack was that I finally understood I needed to build a comfort zone for myself and start focusing on myself as my priority. It took time and effort initially, but—almost overnight—I felt more aligned with my true feelings. I recognized I helped Jack because I'd felt bad for him. I didn't want to be seen as unhelpful. Next time, I'll gracefully bow out.

I felt more at peace, and able to recognize and choose when to step in or out of my comfort zone once I was connected to my feelings and learned what felt comfortable and right to me. I was able to make a sound decision, despite what others might have thought I should do.

Finding my comfort zone changed my life and relationships dramatically. I also became more deeply bonded to myself and connected to others.

Finding Your Comfort Zone

Your body is talking to you all the time, and your mind is full of internal dialog to support the signals your body sends you when you're going outside your comfort zone. This exercise will help you determine the width and breadth of your comfort zone.

Close your eyes and think about a recent decision you've made. Now, imagine the decision scenario you chose. Pay close attention to your physical feelings and how busy your mind feels. Take a deep breath, open your eyes, and write down what you experienced. If you like, rate your level of discomfort on a scale of one to ten with one as feeling no discomfort and ten as feeling a great deal of discomfort.

Next, close your eyes again and imagine a different scenario for that decision and focus on your mind and body's reaction to this alternate vision. Take a deep breath, open your eyes, and write down what you experienced. If you rated your experience above, do it again for this scenario.

Now, consider the two scenarios and your ratings. The scenario that resulted in the least discomfort is within your comfort zone. Being aware of how your body and mind feel when you make decisions provides the support you need to do what's best for you. When you're true to you, you make the most loving choice for everyone. In contrast, when you do something you don't want to do, you and others pay on some level.

You'll build your comfort zone the more you connect with your feelings. Before long, you'll be a pro at identifying what decisions to make and which ones to avoid. You have full control here, and it's up to you to make (and keep) yourself happy.

Take your time with this process. Finding your comfort zone gets easier the more you practice.

CHAPTER 18

ARE YOU AS NICE AS *YOU* THINK?

I'd rather be whole than good.

~ Carl Jung

What if I told you that with all your efforts, all that you do for others, all the ways you juggle and prioritize others' needs (at your expense) that none of your giving comes from a loving and authentic place? Instead, it comes from a much scarier place. People-Pleasing is sourced from fear. It arises from insecurities, negative limiting beliefs, a poor self-image, and a desperate need to be loved and accepted. People-Pleasing isn't about making others happy. It's a self-absorbed, selfish agenda-driven need to be validated.

For years, I thought I was anything but selfish and that doing for others all the time made me kind and generous, warm and caring, compassionate and loving. And above all, it was *selfless*! I didn't understand that what I thought was genuine kindness was more about my need to believe I was valuable and worthy of people's time and love. More important, I didn't know the extent to which I abused myself. Because I wasn't emotionally well enough to depend on myself to make me happy, I looked to others to take care of me.

People-Pleasing behavior results in feelings of emptiness, dissatisfaction, anger, and harsh self-loathing. When we cut off our self-expression and mold ourselves into what we think others want, we abandon our values at a core level, and it leaves us feeling alone and unsupported. People-Pleasing appears to pull in love, but it pushes it away.

The caveat about feeling unlovable is that it can make us appear unloving. Because we fear we don't have what it takes to be loved, we can become insecure and guarded, making us unapproachable and fearful, two qualities that don't exude love. And then, when people don't warm up to us, we feel even more unworthy than before, which has us create thicker shields between ourselves and others.

When we don't choose ourselves first, we aren't aligned with what we desire. Instead, we listen to our internal fears about what will happen if we disappoint others, are rejected, or can't take care of ourselves. We ignore our self-care by taking care of everyone else, which isn't loving to anyone involved. We appear to be loving, but we can't give love to others that we don't have to offer. Over time, we become angry and exhausted. Eventually, we beat ourselves up and blame others for the way we feel. It's how toxic relationships come about.

Turning around People-Pleasing ways means confronting the fear that fuels our behavior. The first step is admitting we do things we don't want to do. The second step is being brutally honest and owning that we do those things because we fear we'll be seen as the (fill in the blank) if we refuse, which we don't want to be. Do these two steps, and we'll be closer to accepting how destructive People-Pleasing is.

My friend Liz recently told me how she felt compelled to support a friend who was undergoing back surgery at a time when Liz barely had any time to spare. Complicating the request was that her friend needed help with activities that could re-injure Liz's back which was recently bothering her.

As Liz was telling her story, she seemed frustrated and angry the more she revealed the details surrounding her friend's request.

I asked, "You're willing to risk hurting your back so that she gets to be careful and not hurt hers? Why are you compromising yourself in this way?"

She looked confused at first but then realized how funny it sounded and how inappropriate and compromising it would be to hurt herself while helping someone else. No one seemed to care about her back, including her.

A moment later, she answered: "I don't want to appear like a bitchy, mean neighbor that doesn't want to help out." She realized that she cared more about how she would be *seen* rather than she cared about helping her friend out.

I've compromised myself many times for another thinking I was such a nice person. I didn't stop to think where my kindness and compelling need to please was coming from. When my anger and frustration got the better of me, I realized I was more afraid of what others thought of me than I was in actually bestowing kindness on them.

Do you wonder why many people think they'll be rejected once others get to know them? This fear is more common than you might think. These folks continue People-Pleasing to avoid being exposed for all the negative things they don't want to be: selfish, angry, mean, phony and so on.

If you want to liberate yourself and live with inner peace, it's best to accept that you're both the dark and the light. As much as you try to hide your dark side, it'll be exposed when you least expect it. If you embrace your dark side instead, you'll have more control over how you behave, and you'll minimize your reactiveness.

By trying to hide the qualities you don't want others to see, you're unknowingly exposing yourself. Have you ever forced a smile when saying yes to something? Your real feelings show in your body language, your energy, your voice, and your face even when you try to hide them. You can pretend that no one knows how you feel, but it's there for everyone to see, feel, or hear.

Years ago, I coached a woman named Lorissa, who had a pharmaceutical sales job that required her to travel to several cities and meet with doctors in well-known hospitals. Since her trips happened every few months or so, she became friendly with some of the staff she visited. One of these people was a prominent pediatrician named Louis.

Louis was a flirt. It was known around his hospital because he flirted with all the pretty nurses. Even though he was in a long-term marriage with children, he didn't lose the opportunity to let women know they were desirable and that he noticed. Lorissa was quite beautiful. She was young, slender, and had a vibrant oval face with soft green eyes and flowing blonde hair. It wasn't surprising that Louis took a liking to her. He didn't hesitate to flirt with Lorissa every time she visited.

During a session, I asked her to find a quality that she didn't like and didn't think she exhibited. Her response was quick and deliberate.

"Mean," she said. "I don't consider myself to be mean."

I replied, "Okay, Let's see if we can find a time in your life when you were mean."

At first, Lorissa was stuck. But then she remembered a visit with Louis in his office when he was coming on more strongly than usual. Lorissa was offended but laughed it off because she felt uncomfortable standing up to him and didn't want to be mean. She confessed that instead of warning him, she went behind his back and reported him to the hospital administration. She learned from a staff member that Louis had been given a warning. She never visited Louis' office again.

Recalling this incident helped Lorissa see that she had a mean part within her. By not confronting Louis, she thought she was hiding how mean she could be. But her mean part came out swinging and led her to go behind his back and humiliate him in a very public way.

The question isn't whether Louis deserved to be reported or not. The issue was whether Lorissa understood that in avoiding being seen as mean, she took action that was, in fact, mean. Her behavior was predictable since, sooner or later, all the qualities we want to hide come out at the least opportune times in our reactions to behaviors we don't like.

Everyone has a mean part. We all have many parts, all the qualities we deem as good and bad. When we embrace that fact and recognize that we can use all our qualities at the appropriate times, we'll accept ourselves more fully and interact with others in healthier ways.

I highly suggest reading Debbie Ford's *The Dark Side of the Light Chasers*, if you want to learn more about integrating your qualities and becoming a whole, emotionally healthy individual. It's certainly the path to freedom and liberation. The information you'll learn will support you in the process of reforming from People-Pleasing, too, because to effectively reform, you must be willing to be seen in a different light. Once you expose and embrace the qualities you don't like and don't want to be, you can use them to serve you instead of sabotage you.

Chapter 19

Loser, Liar, Phony, Fraud

You spot it; you got it!

~ Thomas Merton

Merriam-Webster defines a loser as "Someone or something that loses a game, contest, etc.; someone who is harmed or put in a worse position as the result of something; a person who is not successful, attractive, etc."

Everyone is a loser at one time or another. Sometimes we lose at a game, sometimes things happen in life, and we experience loss, and sometimes we're unsuccessful at the things we set out to do. As I've explained in the previous chapter, it's essential that we own all of the qualities that we possess, the good and the bad. Life becomes liberating when we can be with all of who we are without judging ourselves as wrong and bad. Accepting the loser in ourselves is part of the process.

The Loser

"I could kick myself, I'm so stupid!" said Amy, my client.

As Amy's Coach, I had to sympathize with the pain and shame she felt around not finishing school. I also wanted to support her in making peace with what she didn't want to be: the loser.

I assured her that everyone has a *loser* part. To counteract the loser mentality, you can adopt a *So what?* attitude. As you consider how you became a loser, ask yourself, "So what?" You might be surprised, like Amy was, how losing one thing helped her gain another.

To help Amy explore her loser part more effectively, I asked, "Amy, what was going on in your life at the time you dropped out of school?"

"I didn't know what I wanted to major in. Nothing interested me. I didn't enjoy studying, and I felt confused," Amy replied.

"So..." I prompted

"I took a job in a local restaurant." She started laughing.

Puzzled, I asked, "What's so funny?"

"I get it now. I see that my job at the steakhouse supported me in discovering my love of food and cooking. To this day, I love to entertain, make all my dishes from scratch, and lavish people with beautiful presentations that have them taking out their cameras to photograph their dinner plates!" Amy's excitement was palpable.

"The girl who dropped out of college found her love after all," I said, smiling.

Amy's loser part, the college dropout, helped her discover her love and place in the world. She now understood that sometimes the qualities we don't want to emerge often help us find our way.

Shortly after our session, Amy revealed that she'd signed up for cooking school, something she wanted to do years ago. She was elated that she reconnected with her loser part so she could reconnect to her passion. Today, Amy has a thriving business, teaching people in her community how to cook and throw memorable dinner parties. She's proud of herself and has never forgotten that her loser helped her find her way.

Dennis, another client, considered himself a loser because he couldn't get his business off the ground even after reinventing it several times. After he examined the deeper reasons why it wasn't working, he discovered he lacked passion for the very business he had tried so hard to make work.

Once he opened up to his loser part and stopped making it wrong, he was willing to close his business and try something new. Had he recognized and accepted his lack of passion sooner, he wouldn't have spent so much time and money on a business that wasn't successful.

In time, Dennis found other things he enjoyed and he's now using his creativity to build a business that he believes has a solid chance. He also sees how his loser part has a place in his life, and he'll be paying attention to its influence as time goes on.

I've had plenty of experience with my loser part in relationships. After my third divorce, I realized I was unsuccessful in my primary relationships. I suffered some devastating losses by taking all the responsibility and labelling myself bad and wrong.

I discovered, however, that my losses brought great gifts, too. These gifts supported me in seeing I wasn't there for myself, and that my People-Pleasing behavior was the reason. I had finally opened a door that would turn things around for me.

People Pleasers are the consummate losers. First, they lose their ability to care for their needs and desires and replace them with everyone else's. Then, they repeat this loss in nearly every relationship. The cycle becomes self-perpetuating.

You don't have to dig deep to find your loser part if you're a People Pleaser. Be grateful for the discovery, and don't judge it negatively. Use it to motivate yourself to do things differently and recognize that People-Pleasing is a losing game at attracting love.

The Liar

People Pleasers are often skilled liars. According to Merriam-Webster, "a liar is a person who tells lies" and defines lying as "... marked by or containing untrue statements that are false."

Most People Pleasers believe they're more honest than most, so learning that lying is in their wheelhouse is hard to swallow. The truth is, People Pleasers have no choice but to lie because they're going against many of their true feelings. So as not disappoint anyone, they have to pretend much of the time and make up false statements. They're lying much of the time, especially to themselves.

Saying *yes* when you mean *no*, is a lie. Abandoning your needs and desires is living a lie, as is manipulating the circumstances and people around you to make sure you're loved and accepted. Doing this means you must tell lies.

Don't close this book if you're feeling defensive. It doesn't feel good to think of yourself as a liar, but People Pleasers excel at lying. So, stick with me because accepting and practicing my suggestions will bring you liberation and peace, and allow you to reform from this destructive behavior.

Years ago, I attended a workshop led by the late, Debbie Ford. During one part of the workshop, she was encouraging the attendees to embrace the qualities they disliked about themselves. When she held up the card that read "Liar," one man insisted he *never* lied.

Debbie created several scenarios to help him see that he does lie. Each time, he had evidence that he didn't. His wife of thirty years even stood up and told the room that she could vouch that he doesn't lie.

After a lunch break, Debbie called on this man again.

"Joe, did you ever lie on your tax returns?"

Joe stood up abruptly and yelled with passion, "Young lady, that's another kind of lie!"

The room roared with laughter. Joe sat down looking humiliated. Debbie had finally gotten Joe to see how deeply hidden his liar was. She also encouraged him to embrace this part of himself.

After the workshop, Joe laughed about how difficult it was for him to connect with this part of himself. He shared with everyone how exhausting it was to be so honest and that he was looking forward to using his liar self to be normal like the rest of us.

Please understand that making peace with the qualities we see as negative isn't only for our growth. It's to help us create better relationships with others, too. We'll be more authentic and better able to choose our behavior instead of reacting or overreacting during times when we need to be kinder and more understanding.

If we embrace the notion that everyone is everything, we'll be more compassionate knowing that no one is perfect. We'll make better choices and communicate more directly in asking for what we want and need because fear won't stop us from appearing like a (fill in the blank) when we're confused about something or need to confront someone. We'll use our voice more and be able to set effective boundaries when we need to.

Justifying and rationalizing are two qualities that signal you are likely lying to yourself (and others) as Jennifer's story illustrates.

When my client, Jennifer, first met Larry, she wasn't impressed. Her gut told her that he wasn't the right guy for her. But she continued to convince herself otherwise because, after all, she was in her mid-thirties and frightened that her biological clock was running out of time. She rationalized and justified staying in this relationship. She also admitted that she felt she'd made a mistake by marrying him.

It was hard for Jennifer to own her liar part because she felt she went overboard to please people.

She admitted, "I put up with everything just to be good and make things work out."

Jennifer decided to end her marriage and stop telling the lies she'd told herself and others. She believed bringing children into a bad marriage was worse than having no children, so she was grateful they hadn't taken that step. She still wanted to start a family but knew she had to get out of her relationship with Larry first.

I assured Jennifer that once she was true to herself, she'd know what options are available to her regarding children. By leaving her marriage, she'd have a sound mind with which to make the best choices for herself and her future family.

Sometimes lies are used to protect the feelings of others. When my client, Frank, married Tammy, he told me he didn't love her.

"For years I professed my love to Tammy, but I don't believe I was ever *in love* with her."

Frank felt guilty for not telling Tammy the truth and felt bad for lying.

I asked if he had any intention of leaving his marriage.

He shook his head. "Oh no. I've grown very fond of Tammy over the years, and she's a wonderful mother to our three children."

"Then why do you feel so badly about your feelings?" I inquired.

"I just don't like being dishonest."

I reassured him, "There are lies of all kinds, Frank, and we all lie whether we admit it or not. There are good lies too, I assured him. I explained that if he was honest with Tammy and told her the truth, it would most likely hurt her very much. Also, since he had strong feelings for her and was committed to her, this kind of lie could be considered a blessing.

"How do you think Tammy would feel if she learned you never felt that deep love for her?" I asked Frank.

"She would be destroyed. I believe she loves me very much," Frank answered.

"Don't you think that this is a lie worth maintaining with Tammy then?" I asked.

Frank quickly agreed.

Some lies are acceptable, for example, those that omit painful truths (as in Frank's story). Others that involve betrayal and have a disruptive effect aren't acceptable. Being okay with small lies that avoid hurting someone else means we'll be less likely to tell the big, destructive lies that hurt others deeply.

I hope you're sticking with me here because by owning the parts of yourself you've been denying, you will move toward wholeness. I like to think of it this way. When we reject parts of ourselves, it's like having holes in our bodies. When we find and embrace these parts, we fill in the holes. In that way, we fill ourselves up, and the emptiness that lurks deep within us is replaced with the joy of feeling complete and acceptable. Seeing myself this way truly changed my life in positive ways.

The Phony

Merriam-Webster defines phony as "Not genuine or real, such as intended to deceive or mislead." Not exactly the nicest thing to be, is it? And yet, we all do it. We put on a happy face at one time or another and graciously interact with others for an agenda. Sometimes we mean it and sometimes we don't. When we're knowingly pretending or coming on strong, we're phony. Just like the loser and liar, the phony is a part of all of us, and it's an especially useful persona.

People Pleasers don't realize how skilled they are at being phony. Because the agenda is to be liked at all costs, the People Pleaser must be "on" at all times. To do this requires us to be phony and animated as long as we're interacting with people we're interested in winning over. If you're a long-term People Pleaser, you already know this; you might not feel comfortable admitting it.

I was almost knocked down by the crowd of people that ran toward me in the restaurant.

"Wow!" I said aloud, as I stood up to give my sixty-second info-mercial at a network group I was considering joining. "What a warm welcome from all of you! Thank you!"

I was new in my community and was looking to get out to meet more people, connect, and raise awareness around my business.

When I entered the small restaurant housed in a large office building, I was impressed by the ambiance of the room. I could smell the aromas of something special in the making: steak or chicken teriyaki. The tables were elegantly dressed, and the lighting was soft.

A woman with short blonde hair and an infectious smile greeted me and introduced herself.

I filled out a welcome card, paid twenty dollars for lunch, and was directed toward the rear of the room where some people were gathered. As I walked toward them, some began walking toward me. I looked behind me to see what got their attention and soon realized it was me. To my surprise, they circled me like a school of sharks. With wide grins and hands extended, they all seemed very pleased to meet and greet me. I felt very special.

I forfeited my second option to visit the group before making my final decision. I filled out an application, waited for approval, and joined the group. It felt like a no-brainer.

During my third visit as a member, I got the hang of the required protocol of the group. Each time a guest visited, we, as members, were instructed to make that person feel extra special so they would join. Those who failed to do so would have to put a dollar in the jar that was passed around. The more members, the more referrals, the more money. Now I understood what inspired the friendliness on my first visit. Before long, I was doing it, too. And well, I might add. I understood the reasons why it was important, and we needed great new people to join the group.

Did you spot the phoniness in this story? When we act in ways that may be counter to our normal behavior and with an agenda—in this case garnering new group members—we put on the phony mask.

Are there times in your life when you say things to others you don't mean? These can include:

"Let's do lunch some time."

"I'll give you a call soon."

"Do you have a business card?"

"Let's send referrals to each other."

"Oh, you look gorgeous in that dress!"

"No, I don't think your husband has a roving eye."

"I do think your brother is cute."

"No, you don't look tired."

"I have no preferences."

"No. I'm not angry."

"Nothing's wrong."

"No worries. I can afford this."

All these and other social niceties we use to connect aren't always accurate and honest. We all have times when we're just putting on our gracious hats and pretending.

Be honest with yourself and remove any negative judgment about what you discover. This exercise encourages you to be curious and learn what you do or don't do that brings about the experiences you dislike.

Now, you *can* rationalize and justify all you want to explain away the reasons you don't think you're phony. But if you're willing to recognize how destructive and inauthentic it is not to notice when you're doing it, you'll become outwardly phony, and everyone will see it. You won't become aware of the patterns that sabotage you and your negative experiences will continue.

Some years ago, I hired a trainer to help me learn a routine in the gym that would get me into shape quickly. When I met Carrie, she was pleasant, bubbly, and excited at the prospect of working with me. I told her I was interested in two days per week for four weeks. We made a schedule and met every Monday and Thursday.

I enjoyed my sessions with Carrie; however, she wasn't listening to me. When I broached the subject of learning a routine that I could do on my own, she switched things up leaving me confused about what to do. I brought up my request more than once, but she assured me that she was writing everything down and that I'd have a solid plan to follow.

I felt a little guilty because Carrie was delivering a great deal of value to me in our sessions, and I could sense she wanted to please me. I convinced myself to be grateful and follow along. We were two People Pleasers appeasing each other, which is a fairly common occurrence.

As we neared the end of the four weeks, I saw the opportunity to thank Carrie and move on. But because I didn't have a hold on my People-Pleasing behavior and didn't want to hurt Carrie's feelings, I rationalized that her sessions were inexpensive, and I was getting results in my strength and endurance.

As time passed, Carrie began sharing some personal information about herself. She also gossiped about mutual acquaintances during our sessions. I listened and participated even though I felt it was unprofessional, and it distracted me from my exercises. Before long, I became annoyed and stopped looking forward to my sessions.

Carrie began interrupting our sessions to say hello to newbies in the gym or help someone who was struggling with adjusting a machine. She even ended our session a few minutes early when her next client arrived ahead of schedule. This behavior led me to feel offended and angry.

I once felt that I was an important client and given special treatment. Now I felt taken advantage of. I started watching Carrie closely to observe her behavior with others and me. It didn't take long to see that she was phony and manipulative. I finally decided to end our relationship.

The next day, a mutual acquaintance told me that Carrie had shared some of our private conversations with others. I was furious! It was unprofessional behavior as well as a betrayal between two women. I felt stupid not considering that she was gossiping about me, too, since she was talking about everyone else.

Gossiping is one of the ways People Pleasers engage in interactions. Since they care about everyone liking them, they use whatever angle they can to win as many friends as they desire. They don't see how two-faced, phony, and unkind they're being because they're juggling many people at a time and are preoccupied with being admired. Gossiping also creates a common bonding ground whereby alliances are formed on shared judgments about others.

I was guilty of gossiping, too. But now, I was more upset with myself for not listening to my gut and ending my relationship with Carrie sooner. I felt uncomfortable having to confront her with the feelings I now had, so I decided to be super phony and make excuses to stop working with her. Being phony in this way was useful. It allowed me to hide the real story. I thought it would be an easy conversation; I was wrong.

We met at the pool outside of the gym. Carrie had her usual smile on. I sat down on a chair across from her.

"What's up?" she asked.

"I just wanted to get together and thank you for all your support. I wanted to share in person that I need to stop training. I'm strapped for cash right now and feel comfortable enough to work out on my own," I said.

I didn't expect her reaction. She began to sob so hard that she could barely catch her breath. I sat in shock and felt extremely uncomfortable with her reaction. When she could finally talk, all she did was defend herself. She never once thanked me for working with her for all those months and didn't ask me anything about what I enjoyed or how confident I felt about my progress. This interaction stands as the most unprofessional conversation I've had with anyone. I was horrified.

I could feel the People Pleaser pulling me to say, "I'm sorry" and to hug the woman in distress. But now, I felt an even stronger urge to walk away and let her stew in her stuff. I was beginning to realize that I wasn't responsible for the lousy way she felt about herself. But I held my tongue and spared her the ugly details of why I wanted to get away from her.

I excused myself and left. I spent time mulling over things in my head, a typical activity of People Pleasers. In the end, I believed I did the right thing for myself regardless of the proper way to handle things. I said a quiet prayer for Carrie with the hope that she finds her way. I added that I hoped we both learned from this experience.

The Fraud

Have you ever felt like a fraud? If so, you're in good company. Merriam-Webster defines fraud as "a person who is not what he or she pretends to be." Another way to say this is you're not walking your talk. If this describes your behavior, you might be able to relate to my story.

"You're a fraud!" I declared aloud to myself on a rainy Thursday night. Thankfully, I was home alone.

The year was 2006. I had graduated from the "Institute for Integrative Nutrition" as a Certified Holistic Health Counselor and was counseling clients at my posh New York City apartment. My program consisted of healthy eating tips and ways to overcome emotional eating issues.

I prided myself on being slim, well-dressed, and knowledgeable on the ins and outs of nutrition. And, since I was an emotional eater most of my life, I understood the struggles many of my clients faced around food. I took their success seriously and encouraged them to stick with my program in part because I was a People Pleaser.

After I said goodnight to my last client of the day, I changed into my pajamas, ordered my dinner over the phone, and prepared my favorite martini: straight up with olives.

I relaxed in my elegant living room, the same room in which I advised my clients to become healthier. Sinking into my comfy couch, I relaxed as I drank my martini and smoked cigarettes. All the while, I fantasized about my life and where I saw myself in the future. Once my pizza arrived and I downed three slices, reality hit me hard. This ritual I'd been practicing was feeling increasingly uncomfortable.

"What am I doing? How can I continue this way? This is wrong!" I chided myself in my head.

"You're a fraud!" I blurted out.

I continued to berate myself silently. "How can you counsel people about health during the day and live this contradictory lifestyle at night?"

I had tricked myself into believing that I was walking my talk. I went to the gym every morning, and I kept up on the latest information to share with my clients. But when I opened the windows at night and early the next day to make sure the cigarette smell would disperse, I knew I was hiding something. I didn't want my clients to know what a fraud I was.

This experience changed my life. I had a choice: I give up drinking, smoking, and over-indulging in unhealthy food, or I continue my bad habits and get a new job. Getting a new job was the wrong choice since my heart was invested in helping people, and I'd regret walking away from this opportunity. But keeping my negative patterns in place wasn't serving me either. With that profound awareness, I put out my last cigarette and poured my vodka down the drain. I have never looked back, except to celebrate the night I met my fraud part face-to-face and wonder at how I've experienced so much growth since then.

The greatest lesson was realizing that I was hiding all along. I wasn't okay with what I was doing, and I was ashamed of the part of me that was preaching one thing and doing another. Just like with the loser, liar, and phony qualities, the fraud is part of who we are at various times in our lives. People Pleasers who are continuously deceptive with themselves and others, master these qualities every day unconsciously.

Making Peace with the Loser, Liar, Phony, and Fraud

I'm confident that you can own and make peace with these parts of yourself and accept that as a People Pleaser, you've been honing these skills for years. Once you do, People Pleaser reform will become a breeze, because you want to develop these four qualities healthily to reform. To begin the process, ask and answer the following questions for each quality: loser, liar, phony, fraud. Start by asking, "How have I been <that quality>?" and then identify examples.

Question: How have I been a loser?

Answer: I've experienced loss in my life. I don't finish things. My marriages ended in divorce, etc.

Question: How have I been a liar?

Answer: I've been lying to myself for years about my true feelings. I lie if I want to get out of doing something or need to say no, i.e., I'll say I don't feel good, or I have a conflict. I've lied to people to spare their hurt feelings, i.e., saying you don't look fat in that dress, etc.

Question: How have I been a phony?

Answer: I've put on a happy face too many times to count when I wasn't. I pretend to be okay with some things that bother me and don't let others know about it. I tell people we should get together and then don't call them, etc.

Question: How have I been a fraud?

Answer: I haven't walked my talk at times in my life. I've told others I believed in something I didn't. I preached my opinions and advice when I didn't follow them myself, etc.

Note: This exercise isn't designed to make you wrong or feel bad. It's to help you recognize that we have all qualities: the light and the dark. By embracing the ones you don't want to be, you'll be given a choice as to when to be them. It's also an eye-opening experience into inauthentic People Pleaser behavior.

> **Remember**: *We can't change what we're unaware of and what we don't acknowledge.*

Each quality has a place in your life and can be used in a beneficial way versus a sabotaging way. Learning that you can use these qualities healthily means you won't be hurting anyone, and you'll be closer to getting what you want in life.

I assure you these qualities are utilized when you're People-Pleasing, so why not use them to your benefit? When you hone these skills and use them for your benefit, you'll get what you want, and others will connect with you more effectively. Here's an example to help this sink in.

If I say yes to Irene when she asks me to have lunch when I don't want to, I'm lying to myself and her. I can't do what I want to do, and I become angry with myself. I beat myself up and then later blame her for how I feel. I join her at lunch and don't give her my full attention because I'm preoccupied with not wanting to be there. In avoiding disappointing Irene, I've disappointed myself and been disrespectful toward her.

Let's take the same scenario except Irene asks me out to lunch. I tell her no. She may or may not be disappointed, which I have *zero* control over. I, on the other hand, followed what I needed and wanted. I feel good about myself as a result. I may make up a lie as to why I can't have lunch with her by saying I have a project to do or that I need to pick up my sister. I get to do what I want, I wasn't intentionally hurtful in any way, and I stood up for me. I didn't waste time being where I didn't want to be and didn't use someone else's valuable time being inauthentic and disrespectful.

Use your People Pleaser qualities to help you choose what's best for you. The more you say *no* to others and make yourself your priority, you'll replace the feelings of obligation and become kinder and more generous. Once you take care of yourself and attend to the needs and desires you've neglected, you'll know yourself better and be more willing to serve others in bigger ways.

We're multifaceted beings who desire to be loved and to matter. We seek how to make those things ours, which is how People-Pleasing starts in the first place. We'll do whatever it takes if we believe it will deliver our desired result.

People-Pleasing doesn't work in the long run, so I'm offering you a fork in the road, a way back to the self you may have forgotten. With effort and time, you'll begin to attract the healthy, happy relationships with others you previously used People-Pleasing to find.

CHAPTER 20

SELFISH IS NOT A BAD THING; IT'S THE ONLY THING

"Sometimes you have to be selfish to be selfless."
~ Edward Albert

"I can't hear how busy you are anymore. Either things let up or I'm done!" was the message Ida left on my answering machine after I couldn't oblige her latest requests or continue spending hours on the phone listening to her talk about herself.

I had just started my coaching practice and was getting very busy. I wasn't as available anymore, and Ida was upset about it. My other friends were happy for my success. Her reaction was puzzling.

"If things continue going well, I'll get even busier," I wrote in an email to her. I added, *"I'd have hoped that as my friend you'd be happy and supportive of me."* We didn't see each other anymore after that.

Ida and I met through our mutual friend, Pamela. At first glance, Ida was confident and strong. You could sense this from her firm handshake and her "I've got it all together" persona. She showed up to our first lunch dressed in a soft blue Chanel suit that hugged her slim figure. She carried a Prada bag big enough for the kitchen sink. With her head held high, she walked over to the table. She had an air of importance. I enjoyed our lunch and was intrigued by the executive position she held at a prestigious corporation in New York. We made plans to get together again.

The more time I spent with Ida, the more I began to see her insecurities oozing out from behind her tough exterior. She shared some of her struggles and the disappointing relationships she had with men. I listened intently and gave her some advice when she asked for it.

Before long, Ida was calling more, insisting on picking up the tab for lunches, and buying me little trinkets for no special occasion. I thought she was very nice, but I felt a bit uncomfortable accepting all her gestures. However, she kept insisting. I, being a People Pleaser, obliged her but continued having difficulty accepting the niceties on my behalf.

As time passed, I began sensing troubling vibes during our time together. Ida had an agenda and used her gifts as an upfront payment for my time. And she required a lot of my time. We spent hours on the phone, sometimes in the middle of the night when she'd call me crying about some relationship issue she had with her latest love interest. I'd comfort her and then feel obligated to be there for her because she was so nice to me. In time, my gut began tugging at me to stop and say, "no more."

Before I made my move, I found myself in a financial bind as I waited for the sale of my New York City apartment to close. I needed a large sum of money to take care of some odds and ends. Ida always bragged about her large bank account and offered to help out. I accepted her offer and promised to pay back the money after my apartment sale was finished.

Taking her money only made me feel more indebted to her. Consequently, I made more time for her and allowed my own life to suffer. It was an uncomfortable time in our relationship. I couldn't wait to repay her and was looking forward to asserting myself and making changes in the relationship once I did.

As soon as I received my monies from the real estate sale, I took Ida out to a celebratory thank-you lunch. We met in a posh restaurant and sat at a quiet table in the corner. I handed her the envelope as soon as she sat down.

"Keep it safe," I told her. "It's the certified check paying you back in full for the loan. I am very grateful."

"You know, you don't have to pay me back," she replied matter-of-factly.

I was shocked. I stared at Ida and then said, "I would never take that kind of money from anyone!"

I reiterated my thanks to her for helping me and insisted she take the check, which she finally did.

Despite appearing generous and kind, Ida was manipulative. As long as I was serving her needs and giving her attention and advice, she was giving. As soon as I got busy with work, she withheld. It was a lot of drama.

Our relationship abruptly ended after our email exchange. I thought about the money Ida had lent me and pondered how she could forgive a forty-thousand-dollar loan. I'm sure other people would have taken her up on her offer and then live with the variety of ways she would have made sure they earned it every day.

Today, I understand that Ida was a People Pleaser who desperately needed to be loved. She also craved attention. She was willing to buy what she needed—even friendship. I, too, was accommodating Ida for similar reasons. I needed to be validated and loved, and I looked up to her. I admired her prestigious job and wanted her to like me. I accommodated her to get her approval. I just wasn't aware of it then.

People-Pleasing is selfish and self-absorbed because it's driven by a robust agenda that gives to get. People-Pleasing behavior reflects feelings of insecurity and unworthiness. Thus, People Pleasers suffer from a vampire-like quality of desperation and neediness that sucks the "emotional blood" out of the people they feed on.

As much as the loser, liar, phony, and fraud qualities can be challenging to accept and own at first, 'selfish' is the dirty word that People Pleasers don't want to hear. Avoiding this truth drives People-Pleasing behavior to extreme degrees and creates unhealthy dependency within relationships. If we embrace selfish as an essential quality, teach and preach self-care, our world and our relationships would be the better for it.

Professing that being selfish is wrong, People Pleasers don't take care of their own needs and desires. Sacrifice is the mantra the People Pleaser chants. If they aren't feeding themselves, the only other option they have is to feed off of others in the hopes that those people will see how special the People Pleasers are. It doesn't get more selfish than that.

Since I have a lot of People Pleasers in my life, both family, friends, and clients, I can empathize with their struggles. It's a joy to share with others how to correct the damage that's been done. As much as I screwed up a big part of my life, it's all turned out quite perfect.

Most of all, I recognize that without the proper tools and practices, People-Pleasing can seem like the only choice to get the love you want. The lack of bonding with yourself and the degree of self-loathing that People-Pleasing reinforces leaves the impression that there are no other options. It's not even a consideration.

To experience results from the recommended practices in the previous chapters, you have to do the exercises. There's no easy out for People-Pleasing. It does require work. It's time to own your selfish part and shift the focus to your well-being.

me. I was ready for a boyfriend in my life, and things were looking up. I was happy.

Darryl struck me as genuine and kind, and I trusted him. When he suggested a way to make some easy money each month, I jumped at the opportunity to invest with him. He explained the ins and outs of his business and said he was the middleman between people buying and selling products where everyone makes a profit. Depending on the amount of money you put in, you get back a percentage each month and get the full amount back when the deal matures.

I put in fifteen thousand dollars and received fifteen hundred dollars per month for three months, a 10 percent return on my investment. I had the option of going longer if I wished. I believed I'd stepped into a great deal.

As the maturity date neared, Darryl asked if I would prefer to let the money "ride" and come in on a bigger deal for more money. I agreed and gave him another twenty thousand dollars. I was now all in for thirty-five thousand dollars. I requested something in writing from him just in case, and he gave me a Promissory Note with all the details I asked for. It even contained a clause that he would be responsible for legal fees if needed.

As time went on, my relationship with Darryl changed. He had less time for me. He also spent a good deal of time with his children, whom he had yet to introduce me to. He kept making excuses, and I wasn't buying them. I began to doubt that the relationship was a healthy one for me.

Two months later, Darryl and I had falling out, and I decided to end our romance. I demanded my money back, and he insisted there was a month left on the maturity date and I had to wait. In the meantime, I was angry, frustrated, and scared. I wondered whether I would ever see this money, and I needed it badly. I didn't have a big nest egg.

On the morning the deal matured, I called Darryl on the phone. There was one excuse after another. After a few weeks of stonewalling, I threatened to sue him. Three weeks later, I contacted an attorney and put a few judgments on Darryl's record. When he had trouble renting an apartment, he went ballistic. Darryl was surprised that I took legal action against him. It was my turn to be shocked when my attorney revealed I had fallen for a Ponzi scheme. I wasn't the first person to sue Darryl. I had been dating a con man.

I was so angry at Darryl and myself because I didn't believe something like this would ever happen to me. I believed in us as a couple and thought he wanted to help. I saw the best in people and would always wonder about the dark stories I'd hear others tell. I felt immune to bad things happening to me.

My attorney put together a payment plan that Darryl agreed to pay. It covered the following year, minus any of the interest payments I'd received. Daryl mailed a check every month for eleven months and then wanted to meet in person to deliver the final one since he needed my signature of receipt to remove the legal judgments against him.

Darryl asked if we could meet at the bank. I agreed. Leave it to a con man to think of everything. He didn't trust that I would sign the document. We met at Citibank where he handed me the check. He produced the paperwork and asked for my signature.

"Not until I cash this check," I said. "Have a seat while I go to the teller."

I breathed a sigh of relief with my cash in hand. I had all of my thirty-five thousand dollars back along with a huge lesson to boot.

I sat down next to Darryl and signed his document. He profusely apologized but insisted that his deals were always legitimate and I'd lost out at making some big money. He was a con man to the end.

I looked straight into his eyes and apologized, too, for all the time, love, and attention that he didn't deserve from me. I genuinely thanked him for teaching me one of the most important lessons of my life.

"You were a great teacher for me, Darryl. I will never forget you even though I won't think of you again." And with that, I stood up and walked away.

Even today, many years later, Darryl continues to reach out to me on holidays and birthdays with good wishes. He shares with me how much I taught him and claimed he'll never forget me either. I know that he is a conflicted man, and he's searching for happiness just like the rest of us.

I've asked myself a million times how I could have let this happen. I've always received answers. I often scolded myself for not doing my due diligence and checking Darryl out and for my naivete and lack of experience. Today, my clarity points me to the People Pleaser I was and how I couldn't fathom that people could do the things they do to each other, even though I'd heard these kinds of stories my whole life. My mind did not operate diabolically.

For me, it was about forgiving Darryl and forgiving myself. I learned that boundaries are essential in any relationship. Don't be afraid to ask questions, do research, or be skeptical about people's intentions. It doesn't mean you don't trust; it means you're smart and that others need to earn your trust.

People Pleasers stand on shaky ground when it comes to trusting themselves since their self-doubt is so high. They either become super skeptical or overly trusting with people they know very little about. I believe this is the reason for the many betrayals they attract. It's not enough they defeat themselves with this behavior. Their insecurities and poor self-image invite many more scenarios to convince them of how undeserving they are. Each offense eats away at their low self-worth.

In my People-Pleasing heyday, I was sending mixed messages all the time because I had to be "on" at all times, which meant dismissing my true feelings. If I got annoyed or angry, I had to brush it away to put on a happy face for appearance's sake. Today, we often hear two popular People-Pleasing mantras: "No problem" or "No worries" as short responses to let others know that it's all good when in fact, many times it isn't.

If you're like me and many of my clients, you'll agree that people can take advantage of your time, efforts, and love without giving it a second thought. We have to own, too, that we're guilty of taking advantage of others as well. All relationships are cocreated.

Most people are unaware that we're creating our experiences, good and bad, all day, every day. When we feel unacknowledged and unappreciated for all that we do, we likely make it mean that it's never enough or we're not enough. We're not setting boundaries.

This is how hope diminishes. We do and do and do some more. We go around in circles feeling overwhelmed, frustrated, and disappointed, and then begin to see how others are taking advantage of our kindness. Resentment builds up, and we become angry, sad, and just plain tired of it. Then, we point our fingers at others blaming them for the lousy way we feel. Again, we have no boundaries.

If we send the proper messages to others demanding basic respect and consideration, we'll get it. Make no mistake; people are generally willing to oblige. It's just that they don't know what we want. We're the ones who must determine the outcome based on what we believe we deserve. Then, we must communicate what that is to others.

Of course, you must be clear about what you need and want. But sometimes you might feel confused and frustrated when people don't get the right message about you or your needs and desires, like my friend Robbie. She's not been able to get what she needs from her husband, Don.

Robbie and I met up after Christmas. Her frustration about the gift from her husband was obvious.

"He just doesn't get it," she said with frustration. "That's the ring I would love, I told him. I took him into the store two different times and pointed it out. I even had the salesgirl write down the name for him," she said. She continued, "There I was on Christmas morning, gleaming with excitement as I unwrap the small jewelry box, believing he finally came through."

I could tell by the look on her face that things hadn't turned out as she planned.

She looked at me and said, "Does Don not care? Why is nobody listening to me? Why can't I just get what I want already?"

"So, what happened?" I asked.

Don got me a beautiful ring. It was a ring he liked more than the one I picked. It was nice, and it was more expensive, too. I felt ashamed after I threw it at him and ran out of the room. I'm just tired of not getting what I want. Her eyes filled with tears.

I asked, "What stopped you from thanking Don and returning the ring for the one you wanted? Couldn't you let him know that you still preferred to get what you asked for instead?"

She was confident in her answer, "Because I already told him what I wanted. He just chose to do otherwise."

I knew that Robbie was a People Pleaser and that People Pleasers have a difficult time being assertive and demanding. They believe it's wrong to tell others what they need, and instead choose to send out clues to hint at what they want. And because this time Robbie was more direct by showing Don the ring she wanted, she felt rejected that he didn't honor that request.

These situations can deeply hurt because the People Pleaser already feels cheated. They're putting their needs and desires aside to please others. After enough times, they're just burned out and tired of it all. They can now seem impatient and intolerant to others when they've hit their boiling point. All the resentment they've been holding in explodes. They feel disappointed, uncared for, and blame others for not appreciating them. This situation frequently occurs in relationships, and it's toxic.

People Pleasers need to set boundaries that let others know what is and isn't okay. They need to be willing to feel the discomfort to speak up and ask for what they need.

I assured Robbie that her request was new and that Don didn't take it seriously because most of the time she enabled Don to do what he wanted. Sometimes it takes repetition or setting several boundaries before our partners get the message.

I remember a similar situation during my first marriage.

We were approaching our ten-year anniversary, and I wanted to reset my engagement ring by adding some stones and changing the setting. Daniel had his eye on a watch he had picked out for me and suggested we spend the money there.

"Why don't you just buy me a box of chocolates," I retorted. "And when you want to get me what I want, then we can talk." I was insulted and reactive.

Like Robbie, years ago I expected people to know what to do to make me happy. I believed I shouldn't have to ask. I would think, "He should know by now. If he loves me, he would know how to treat me."

That phrase was my mantra. I laugh at myself today because I don't think I even knew what would make me happy then. I left it all to chance and to others to take care of me, while I was taking care of everyone else but me. I had the notion that soon some knight in shining armor would save me. I believed that to get what I want in life, someone had to give it to me.

That was a hard lesson to learn. Today, I now know for sure that no one is coming and that to live an extraordinary life, I alone have to claim my right to it. Whereas knowing this in the past would have destroyed me, today it liberates me because I know I have more control than I ever had back when I was People-Pleasing.

I urge you to wake up to the fact that every one of us is responsible for our well-being. Any other way of living is a lie. Since we've been misguided and deceived by others who taught, modeled, and encouraged us that People-Pleasing is the way to be, we've just followed along like good students and heeded the lesson that created destruction in our lives. We must unlearn how we've operated with others, find our course correction, and make positive changes.

It sounds easier said than done. It's a catch-22 because we've been doing what we believed is right, which hasn't been working, so we step up the behavior thinking we're not doing enough. Increasing the behavior makes things worse, which causes us to dislike ourselves even more. Finally, we've no other choice than to continue the behavior because we can't rely on ourselves.

My mission is to support you and others to recognize that by making yourself the priority and letting go of People-Pleasing behavior, you'll fill yourself up and serve others in much bigger ways.

People-Pleasing behavior that suggests sacrificing ourselves in the name of others' needs defeats what we're all here for, which is to bestow our unique gifts on others and the world so that our planet benefits from our presence here. We can't do this by abandoning ourselves.

When we take care of ourselves first, it becomes a natural desire to do for others. When we fill ourselves up, we're in the position to impact and inspire others in ways People-Pleasing can never do.

My intention in this chapter is to support and encourage People Pleaser reform as the *only* path to reclaiming the self you've lost in the pursuit to make others happy. I believe it's the only answer to living a fulfilling, happy life while interacting with others in healthy ways.

A giant step in that endeavor is setting boundaries, demanding respect and being forthright with others about what you need and want. It's the only way you'll reach the point of integrity that allows you to respect yourself and stop blaming others for the way you feel.

The recommended practices I've shared in previous chapters were designed to get you ready and committed. Now, it's time to take radical action if you're serious about putting an end to the destructive, futile behavior of People-Pleasing and embark on the path of reform.

It's time to come back to you and be clear about what you truly desire in life. You can't fully know this until you understand and bond with *you*.

This work requires that you learn to trust yourself. I emphasize the term *learn*. People Pleasers are full of self-doubt because of their insecurity and low self-worth. This work also requires you to rely on your gut and intuition to direct your choices and actions, the voice you've been pushing away to listen to the demands of others. It also requires that you shift the fear from what scares you into doing all the things you don't want to do to avoid loss or hurting others, to seeing the worst-case scenario of what will happen if you don't stop: a life unrealized.

Take a deep breath. Reform requires that you trust no one but yourself for a while. You must focus and listen only to you when it comes to determining your choices and actions. You must rely solely on yourself and not ask for feedback from others.

If you're seeing a therapist or a coach for support during this process, by all means, listen carefully to their encouragement but make sure that you give your voice equal credence as to the direction you want to go. Even professionals don't know what's best for you and your life, only you do.

If you're married, in a business partnership, or in a relationship where you have investments, you must still hear your voice first, and it must be the voice of certainty for you. If you allow others' voices to overwhelm you, you won't learn how to trust yourself.

The reform process requires a complete focus on you. To get back the "self" that you've lost through People-Pleasing, you must be your only source for choices and decisions until you're grounded and listening to your guidance without doubting yourself when receiving feedback from others.

Once you're bonded to yourself and trust yourself as the right source for your life's decisions, then it's your choice as to whom you open up to and trust. Your internal guidance will let you know what feels right. My highest recommendation is that no one gets the benefit of the doubt without earning it. If I had known this wisdom earlier in my life and followed it, I would have spared myself a lot of grief and struggle. I know it now, and I know it for sure. There's nothing wrong with being careful and a little guarded. Follow your instincts.

Once you put the spotlight on you, the first step in boundary setting is to ask yourself what kinds of messages you want to send in your relationships. Forget for a minute how you would do it and ask what it is you want from others and what you want them to understand about you. Below are examples to help you get started.

What I Want from Others is...

Respect and consideration.

Loyalty.

Trust.

To listen to what I have to say.

To keep promises.

To let me know if I've offended them.

To let me know what they need.

This list can be as long as you'd like. I suggest the longer, the better so that you get to know more about what you need and want.

The next list is about the messages you want others to know so that they're clear about what's okay and not okay with you.

The Messages I Want Others to Know are...

It's not okay to talk down to me or in offensive and inappropriate ways.

It's not okay to break promises.

It's not okay to deceive me in ways that are hurtful.

It's not okay to tell me you will call and then don't.

It's not okay to assume I know how you feel.

Make your list as long as possible because it will help you gain clarity about what you want others to know.

The last list includes the boundaries and consequences you'll set for yourself and others to stay in integrity and to relinquish your People-Pleasing behavior. I suggest that you set boundaries and consequences in partnerships where you have a large personal investment, i.e., a business partnership and marriage before you enter into them and as issues arise. In all other relationships, deal with things as they arise and handle them accordingly. I'm not married or in a business partnership, but if I were, below are examples of the boundaries and consequences I would set.

Boundaries in Relationships (Business Partnerships and Marriages) I must have are...

Mutual disclosure on any important decisions and choices.

Mutual respect and loyalty, and to have each other's back.

Confidentiality and keeping the relationship sacred.

No offensive, condescending, or disrespectful communication.

Timely sharing of displeasure with the other instead of holding resentment.

Make your list as long as possible to create realistic and solid boundaries.

Consequences for Not Adhering to Boundaries

For large betrayals, i.e., breach of contract, infidelity, etc., my preference is to end the relationship. I find it difficult to effectively give to relationships where there's a lack of trust. For me, it's a deal breaker. In my past, I reconciled with several people under these circumstances and found it to be detrimental to myself and my integrity. How you choose to handle large betrayals is up to you. It never hurts to put things in writing, i.e., contracts, riders to contracts, etc.

People will come and go in our lives, and large betrayals can be the demarcation point where exits are appropriate. Remember, with losses, lessons stick. Also, if you choose to leave the relationship, it doesn't mean you can't forgive. I believe forgiveness is essential to moving on. But remember, giving more is not recommended. If you remain in the relationship, be cautious and withhold your trust until it's earned. You don't want to reward bad behavior. Otherwise, you could fall into the repeat-offender category, which is self-abusive. For the breaking of other boundaries, I suggest you talk with the other party and withhold whatever feels right to you until they earn your trust again and have apologized to you.

You'll know the right boundaries and consequences to set the more you focus on your needs and desires. You'll know what your deal breakers are and what you will or won't tolerate. Remember, the boundaries and consequences others set with you must be followed and taken seriously, too. Just as we teach others how to treat us, we should treat others as they wish.

In addition, I want to caution about how to confront and communicate with others while going through the reform process. Remember, your welfare needs to come first. You want to protect your feelings always as well as your sanity. It's important to note that some relationships are toxic and added communication could leave you vulnerable to more stress and disappointment and deter your forward progress.

I used to believe that if I just made others understand how I felt, they would see things the way I did. I know now this isn't true. Many of us have people in our lives who deflect responsibility and are skilled at pointing the finger at anyone but themselves. You're probably nodding your head in agreement and know who these people are. If you're not invested with people like this, I suggest walking away with as little an explanation as possible or even none at all. You don't have to start up a conversation or take their calls. Sooner or later, people get the message. While it's nice to have mutual respect, it's just not possible with some people.

Walking away may appear cowardly or unfair, but I suggest embracing the coward because there's often less anxiety with cutting people off. Some people won't get the message without making you the bad guy. You'll likely know this ahead of time depending on the offensive behavior they've shown you. You've probably already experienced many conversations with these people where they either don't hear you or see their part in anything. Don't diminish your energy to give them closure. They most likely don't or won't understand, and then you'll be left pulling out your hair. Give yourself closure and let them worry about theirs.

If you want to move on from people who have treated you with respect in the past and have owned responsibility for their actions, have a conversation with them. But don't overshare. People Pleasers are famous for oversharing and explaining themselves. Because they don't feel worthy of their right to their feelings, they talk around them and then explain, explain, explain to feel validated.

When you're invested in a relationship such as a marriage or business partnership and you are no longer willing to stay in the relationship, be clear about your decision before broaching the conversation. Be sure you know your reasons why. If you're throwing the divorce word around or threatening to break a contract, you may scare the other person and then there may be no other recourse. So, be sure.

Always take measures to protect yourself and recognize that once you sever a relationship with another who invested in you, the dynamic can become oppositional quickly. Protect yourself and say just enough to give your reasons and intentions. The separation becomes more complicated if children are involved. You'll remain in each other's lives, so it's best to keep a good relationship going so you can mutually parent your children. Make sure you have legal representation regardless. If it's a business partnership, you'll want to be represented legally as well and be careful what you disclose.

I hear so many of my friends and clients describe how they're parting on friendly terms. I caution them to be aware and careful that you don't always know what the other is thinking or doing. When lawyers get involved, it can get contentious, so make sure you don't get the wool pulled over your eyes.

During this time, it's important to trust yourself. Make the decisions and choices that feel right to you and know that you are your greatest supporter and protector. Most of all, recognize that you are entitled in your relationships. People Pleasers step over their rights.

It may feel uncomfortable at first because People Pleasers forget this vital information. It's going to be up to you to claim the life you want. Now is as good a time as any.

CHAPTER 22

SAYING NO WITH PASSION

No is a complete sentence.

~ Annie Lamott

At two years old we were saying *no* often, with passion and with the innocent knowing that we're meant to stand up for ourselves and defend our needs and desires. We were connected with ourselves then even if we couldn't make sense of how or why. We knew on some level that we had a choice.

Even though we were clueless about all the drama, trauma, and struggles that lay ahead for us, we exercised our voices loudly. Before long, we got the message that doing so wasn't okay. We then started separating from ourselves and began People-Pleasing. We let go of the most powerful word in our vocabulary: *No.*

It's sad when people say they went against the essence of who they are and what they're meant to do to please a parent, support a family, or make better money. Many are living the *should* life. Not disappointing others becomes more important than taking care of the self. Saying no to others becomes difficult for the People Pleaser who knows all too well that it's not a good idea to disappoint others.

I have a friend named Ron who struggles every day. You can't tell because he puts on a happy face and aims to please. He's very busy avoiding his feelings.

"My problems aren't as bad as others," he insists. "God only gives you what you can handle, so I'm assuming mine is hardship."

"I guess it's admirable to be so positive," I said. "But, where do you think you'll end up when you're old and gray if you don't 'fess up to how you really feel?"

Ron is married to Sally who has chronic fatigue syndrome. He loves his wife and twin sons very much but admits his life is impaired by his wife's illness. He's young and virile, and he can't remember the last time they had sex. I can tell from looking into his eyes that he's extremely sad.

When we make vows and promises, they can cloud the way forward, especially when significant challenges arise that don't have easy answers. I believe that we're entitled to be happy, and sometimes that means making decisions that leave the future uncertain. But it can be hard to determine what is the best and most loving choice for everyone involved when we're miserable. When do we start saying no and no more?

Everyone has their own stories about adversity and hardship. I believe many of us end up in predicaments because we don't fight for what we want. We deceive ourselves and others into thinking we're okay with the way things are, which may seem admirable, but it's a lie. Sooner or later, everyone pays.

I've coached countless clients who've stayed in relationships that didn't feel good because of guilt or shame and not wanting to hurt others. Then, before long, the person they stayed with asks for a divorce. My clients become angry because they didn't consider their happiness and their partner wasn't willing to ride out the rollercoaster on their behalf.

Please recognize that if you're unhappy in your relationship, the other person probably is, too.

Ron's wife Sally is understandably absorbed in her illness. But she's unwilling to do anything to change the situation in their marriage.

"I didn't ask to get sick," she said. "Things are just the way they are," is the tune she sings.

Does Ron accept this and stay for the children and the marriage? Or, does he seriously consider leaving and addressing his happiness?

When is it time to start saying no to others and yes to yourself? What limit do we have to reach before we've resigned ourselves to an unhappy life? What's the most loving thing to do?

When we feel a strong physical *no* to anything we do, and we don't honor it by taking measures to address it or change things, our lives can fall apart quickly. Whether it's following in your parent's footsteps to become a doctor when your heart yearns to be an artist, staying in a marriage that feels like a prison, continuing a friendship with someone who brings you down, or compromises and violates you, the people in your lives will be affected, too. It's just a matter of time before it shows.

My client, Robert, is an avid People Pleaser. He's accommodating and always aims to please. He also goes ballistic when other cars cut him off on the highway. It's safe to say he's holding a lot of anger. His reactions confuse him, because he doesn't want to react or be angry, and he doesn't fully understand that he's not allowing himself to feel what he feels.

Robert has a hard time saying no to the women he dates. If he meets a woman who likes him but in whom he's not particularly interested, to avoid hurting her feelings, he tells her what she wants to hear. He carries on the relationship feeling uncomfortable and miserable. When it becomes unbearable, he becomes inconsistent and inconsiderate. He doesn't return calls or texts and goes missing in action.

He insists this isn't how he wants to be. "I don't want to say no and hurt their feelings either. I end up talking myself into believing that

I can make it work with them, but I know my heart's not there. I don't want to disappoint them."

I asked him, "Don't you think they'll be more disappointed after investing their time and heart with you and learning later that you don't feel the same way?"

"I see your point," he replied, nodding. "I guess I just have to 'fess up."

"If you understand it's more loving to be upfront and not lead them on, then it should be an easy choice," I said. "You have no control if people get disappointed. You do have control over whether you get disappointed."

He turned thoughtful. "I guess, too, there's sometimes I'm scared of being alone, and so I force the relationship."

"Now we're getting somewhere," I said. "Is it that you don't have faith you'll find someone you like or that likes you?"

"Yes! That's it!" he shouted.

People Pleasers have a lot of fear that they'll never get what they want in life. So they force themselves to be with what is and resign themselves to life not working out for them.

It's up to all of us to start saying no to what doesn't feel good because we're the only ones who can do that for ourselves. We can't continue being so arrogant as to think that others can't survive without us or that there are no solutions to our problems. We must be true to ourselves and stay in integrity with our truth; otherwise, it's a matter of time before we overreact to something and sabotage ourselves.

"You made your bed; lie in it," my father used to say often. He was miserable, and it affected the whole family. No one was happy as a result, and my sister and I wished our parents would divorce.

When I was a young teenager, I was rooting for the breakup. Instead, they stayed together for their children. We regularly suffered because of their dysfunction.

After my sister and I were grown, my father built a second kitchen so that he and my mother could live in the same house but each had space of their own. In time, he bought another home to fully separate from my mother. They continued to talk and meet for dinner sometimes because I believe my father was lonely and felt responsible for taking care of my mother. But there was no joy, and there was no love. It was enmeshment and dependency created by insecurity and self-loathing on both their parts.

My parents were amazing, good, and decent people who deserved to be happy and live full lives. I'm sad that this wasn't how they lived. There's no greater tragedy than a life unrealized, not deeply knowing yourself, and loving who you are. When we don't live in alignment with our heart's desires, we die in many ways. We become disconnected, depressed, fearful, apathetic, hopeless, disillusioned, and resigned. Some go further, becoming angry, bitter, and resentful.

These dark, emotional nudges give us vital information and alert us that we're not living our desires. We've all heard of the proverbial wake-up call. These feelings shake us into awareness. That's why the word *no* is the game changer in your life. You say it to yourself daily whenever you compromise and sacrifice your needs and desires. There will always be things we don't want to do but choose to do; however, there's a difference between taking responsibility and abandoning yourself in the process.

I invite you to use your power and start saying *no*. *No* is a complete sentence. Below are phrases to help you feel comfortable saying *no*.

Ways to say *No*

"No, I can't.

"No, I have a conflict."

"No can do."

"No, not now."

"No, it doesn't work for me."

"Gosh no, the timing is off."

"No, I have to work."

"No, I have a prior commitment."

"No, I have a doctor's appointment."

Be creative with your responses. Create whatever excuses work for you. It's time to devise a few untruths that support you in getting out of a commitment you don't want to make without hurting anyone's feelings. Remember, you don't have control over others' feelings, behaviors, actions, or reactions. People get disappointed, no matter how much you try to avoid it.

Saying *no* is necessary if you want to live a happy life. It's a game changer because it shifts the responsibility onto you to claim your rights and call the shots. You may feel uncomfortable with this responsibility at first, but you'll become a pro at it in no time. You'll probably kick yourself for not doing it sooner.

CHAPTER 23

THE AFTERMATH OF REFORM

The true profession of man is finding his way to himself.

~ Hermann Hesse

There's a gift in hitting rock bottom. There's nowhere left to fall, and for many of us, it's the only time we stand up and seek support. It's also the perfect time to choose change and implement the effort and practices required to produce success.

The recommendations I've suggested to support reform have worked beautifully in my life and in the lives of clients and friends who've experimented with my exercises. They rave about their results. I hear the word "liberating" a lot.

Your commitment, time, attention, willingness, effort, patience, tolerance, and trust are crucial. Initially, when you start taking on these practices, you'll experience confusion, anxiety, and trepidation—all the feelings you're familiar with while People-Pleasing. You may feel as if the Universe is testing you by creating a new and unfamiliar sort of struggle. Please know these feelings are temporary. Whenever we break a pattern or addiction, there's a period of withdrawal and adjustment. Just continue to be kind and compassionate with yourself, and this phase will pass quickly.

Rest assured, your fear and doubt, your feelings of loss, as well as the plethora of emotions that come up during the reform process are indicators of a shift. It can feel good and unfamiliar at the same time. Stick to your commitment to bond with yourself, and you'll be greeted with renewed confidence, hope, possibility, and limitless opportunities once you've made yourself the priority in your life.

I was lying on my bed on an ordinary Friday night, deciding what to watch on television. I felt a sense of peace I'd not felt in many, many years. I was deeply relaxed. My mind wasn't spinning in circles, and I wasn't ruminating about what happened during the day or what was to come tomorrow.

This is what it must feel like to experience the present, I thought.

Instead of feeling overly excited or overwhelmed about the intense feelings that came up for me, I felt a contentment that seemed to stay with me without thinking about it or trying to create it. It was similar to what I would feel early in relationships where I was falling in love, and things looked promising for my future. I remember those times as feeling at peace, safe, and secure as if I was wrapped in a warm, protective embrace. I consciously felt alive instead of analyzing how I was living. All judgments were silent as if there was nothing to adjust or change, nothing to care or worry about. All I felt was love.

In my past relationships, the feeling of being connected and loved wouldn't last, because I was People-Pleasing and depending on others to feel good about myself. Circumstances were always changing. I always felt out of control and dreading that an imaginary ball would drop to destroy any happiness I had. With new demands came self-doubt and fear around losing the relationship.

Now, lying on my bed surrounded by my two beautiful dogs, I felt blessed and complete.

"Gosh. This is what self-love must feel like," I mused.

I felt genuine gratitude for myself and how far I've come. I don't think I'd ever deeply acknowledged myself by just being still. It was a new feeling for me. Nirvana is the only word that comes to mind to encompass the quietude and lack of effort it took to feel completely happy.

I wondered, *Is this the inner peace and balance I'd always been seeking?*

I was convinced that if I could reach this state of bliss, I could teach others to do this for themselves, too. This realization sparked the inspiration to write this book and why I have committed to writing other books as well. There is so much to say.

As I traced back to the first steps I took toward reforming from People-Pleasing, I knew that being with my darkest feelings helped me break through to the light. I stopped resisting my anger, sadness, and shame.

A few years ago, I attended a workshop in Florida with the late Dr. Wayne Dyer. He was telling a personal story about driving thousands of miles to take a piss on his father's grave. In only the way Wayne Dyer could tell a story, he had the audience laughing and crying at the same time. After resenting his father for years for abandoning him as a toddler and leaving his mother penniless with other children to feed, he set out to visit his deceased father's grave to give him a piece of his mind.

After screaming obscenities at the tombstone as he checked off a list of resentments he blamed his father for, Wayne headed back to his car, closed the door, turned on the ignition, and then realized he forgot to piss on the grave. He reached for the door handle, and then he froze. He was suddenly overcome by intense emotion. He started to cry. Through his tears, he had a profound epiphany. "Who am I to judge this man?" he asked. He knew nothing about his father's life, his childhood, or how he might have suffered. How could he judge his father and yet not understand the journey he lived through? A sense of forgiveness flooded his body, which helped him to make peace with the man who'd abandoned him. The story was incredibly moving and demonstrated that a breakdown is necessary before a breakthrough.

I resonate with this story because my journey to reform from People-Pleasing began with acknowledging my anger and disappointment without censoring myself with rationalizations or justifications. I knew I carried tremendous anger that needed to be released. You can't forgive what you don't feel, own, or acknowledge.

I'd always avoided getting in touch with my anger. Even when I ranted and raved, and stood up in my defense, deep down I didn't believe my anger was acceptable, and I didn't feel entitled to it. I'd rehash stories with people unconsciously seeking their validation that I had a right to my dark feelings. When I understood that my anger was a valid part of me, I completely accepted it. I spewed a litany of grudges and resentments that still lingered within me. I heard myself shout, *"No more! Not ever again!"*

My declaration that I would no longer compromise or violate myself voluntarily for anyone or anything was my form of revenge. As poet George Herbert once said, "Living well is the best revenge." It gave me the fuel to clean up and resolve issues with the people and things I held residual anger for. It was a cathartic process.

While you're reforming, it's critical that you find ways to channel your feelings. It may also be necessary to withhold from others until you can strike a balance between giving to yourself first and then giving to others. I'm not suggesting that you abdicate responsibility for children or others who depend on you, but I am suggesting that you stop volunteering or allowing others to ask favors of you during this time. You can't reform from People-Pleasing while People-Pleasing. Using this sacred time to bond with you and putting others' needs aside is key. Those who care about you will be there when you're ready. Those who don't care were most likely using you, and it might be beneficial to know who they are. You can always revisit the exercise of compartmentalizing the people in your life and place people properly in or out of your life.

Releasing your anger and sadness is essential for your healing. The exercise below will assist in this process.

Feeling and Releasing Your Anger

A simple way to feel and release your anger is to get angry and use movement to help shift your energy while you voice your feelings. Try the following:

Beat on a pillow

Go all out on a punching bag

Lock yourself in your car and scream at the top of your lungs

Throw and break glass safely (Some places allow this now.)

Kick cans in the backyard

Dance to hard rock

These are some of my suggestions to release anger. Discover what works best for you. As long as you're not hurting yourself or anyone else, these are safe, effective ways to act out the emotions that live within you.

Feeling and Releasing Your Sadness

Here are a few options for getting in touch with and releasing your sadness.

Play old songs

Have a good cry

Journal about your sadness

Watch a sad movie

Discover what works best for you.

Once the anger and sadness move through you, you'll experience a quiet, neutral feeling as these emotions dissipate.

Once you've done this exercise, and you feel you've released your anger and sadness, you can then spend your valuable time bonding with you.

The reform process is a journey that takes patience and time. Make space to reflect on and become familiar with yourself so that you can discover your needs and desires. Doing this is especially important if it's difficult for you to be by yourself. You will learn a great deal, and it'll speed up your progress. You may also find that once you're more comfortable and grounded with yourself, the fear of being alone will subside.

Keep reminding yourself that People-Pleasing hasn't brought happiness into your life, that it hasn't worked, and it has brought you little to no return on investment. Does it make any sense to continue doing it?

Even at the earliest stage in the reform process, you'll begin to feel secure and confident seeing yourself as a support for you. Hold the vision that you're finding your way to your heart's desires and that this process will fill you up and position you to know yourself so that you can serve the world.

As with any radical change or reinvention, you may feel as if you're not firmly grounded in place. You've entered the space between your commitment to stop People-Pleasing and the full benefits of reform. I call this Limbo Land. It's a nowhere zone where you're not your old self, but you're not fully reformed yet either. I encourage you to use your time in this space to be kind and compassionate with yourself and know that you're feeling your way through it. This stage is short. Stay proactive and acknowledge yourself daily for your commitment and your progress, resist any negative judgments about yourself or where you are in the process, and keep strong practices in place. Limbo Land can even be a peaceful respite from all the drama and overdoing you were once used to. Breathe and relax.

I also encourage you to refer back to this book, continuously doing the recommended practices, and surround yourself with resources that will help you heal.

As my gift to you, I have created a compilation of resources I swear by. You can obtain this gift by going to my website: www. LessonsLearnedInLove.com. Add your name and email address in the specified box to receive access to the downloadable document, "Crazy, Blissful, Happy: A Compilation of Resources to Get You High on Your Life." I also encourage you to visit my website, www. PeoplePleasersReformAcademy.com and join for free. You can also check out my private Facebook page with the same name, where I post seven days a week.

Please keep acknowledging yourself for all the progress you're making and for the desire and willingness you have to change your life from People-Pleasing to *extraordinary*. Your commitment to focus on knowing you will support you to support others in ways People-Pleasing could never do. Instead of being interested in people for how they feel about you, you'll be interested in people for who they are, and you'll be eager to learn all about them.

In the chapters ahead, you'll learn how reform will lead you to your life's purpose, what it takes to create an extraordinary life, and what's next after you finish this book.

Please note: By reading this entire book, you'll learn the benefits of People Pleaser reform, which will, hopefully, motivate you to make a continued commitment to the process. You may also need to revisit this book periodically to refresh your memory and rededicate yourself to People Pleaser reform.

CHAPTER 24

DISCOVERING YOUR LIFE'S PURPOSE

The mystery of human existence lies not in just staying alive, but in finding something to live for.

~ *Fyodor Dostoyevsky*

As I walked my dog Tabitha one morning, I pondered the difference between a *purpose* and a *calling*. I thought back to how creative I became after I screwed up the prime years of my life by taking the dangerous path of drugs. I contemplated the myriad bad decisions I'd made and how those resulted in panic attacks in my forties that motivated me to make some radical changes.

After my third divorce dropped me to my knees in my mid-fifties, I was faced with two choices. I could resign myself to life not working out and continue going through the motions while moping in secret, or I could use all the drama and trauma for the betterment of my life and then share it with others. I chose the latter. When life gives you lemons, you make a sour face, and then you make lemonade.

I believe our purpose is about using our journey, regardless of how our lives unfold. We make sense of that journey and support it positively. Anything can be turned into a purpose, especially adversity.

For some people, their purpose and calling are the same. These people recognize their dreams early, go after them, and live them. For most of us, our early calling in life may not be realized. No matter. We can still live a happy, purposeful, passionate life.

Today, I live my purpose as an emotional wellness coach supporting others to embrace and love who they are and jump into life with both feet. Of course, People Pleaser reform is dear to my heart and usually part of their process.

As Tabitha and I turned the corner, I wondered what my calling could be? I thought back to when I was a little girl and remembered the things I loved before I became a People Pleaser—before I became invisible. I loved to twirl and dance. I loved to laugh. I focused on happiness and love. I worked diligently to get my family members connected. I enjoyed peace and serenity. Was being a dancer my true calling? Was having a happy family with children my calling? If either was my calling, I missed them both.

I thought, "I feel very happy. I am happier now than I've ever been before in my life. How do I account for my newfound joy and peace? Isn't this a calling of sorts?"

I considered that I no longer woke up in the morning with a surreal sense that I was disconnected and merely going through the motions of life as I waited for something unknown to show up. I was curious as to what produced that shift. These days, I awaken each morning refreshed and excited to start my day. What could account for my peace and joy?

I had experienced tremendous growth after committing to reform from People-Pleasing. I knew my answer was hidden within that process. Writing this book was cathartic, and it allowed me the time to unravel many profound epiphanies including the one I'm about to share with you.

As Tabitha and I came upon our front door, I stopped in my tracks. I could *see* the answer to my question: I saw myself as a young girl who loved to write but who later stopped when life got hard. It seems I'd found my calling after all. It began unfolding once I stepped deeply into the process of writing to expose the dangers of People-Pleasing and how it created havoc in my life. To write required me to remember who I was before I abandoned myself. In my mind's eye, I could see that young girl again. What a welcome sight!

Just a few weeks ago, I declared to everyone in my life that I've decided to write more books. I have a lot to say and much to share. I'm happy when I am writing. And my younger me is with me every keystroke, every word, and every sentence. She's helping me write about the hard things in life. What a hoot!

In the end, life is all about love, connection, and deep meaning. No matter where your journey has taken you, there's always a path inviting you to return to what you once loved. You have a life worth living. Embrace your calling.

Finding your purpose and calling in life requires you to listen carefully to yourself. Doing so becomes easier as you continue reforming from People-Pleasing. The more you say *no*, the more you stay true to your needs and desires, the more you take really good care of you, the more you honor yourself as a special friend, your purpose and calling will find you. You'll know when it finds you because you won't question it. It will just feel right.

As long as you're willing to feel and be with all of your feelings, you're on the right path. Stop minimizing or glossing over what eats away at you. I stayed stuck for years because I was avoiding my anger. I was living the *should* life, and it was driving me crazy. Stuffing away my expression as not to make waves with others caused me much anxiety and didn't bode well in relationships.

Once you honor your feelings, you can open up to your voice and expression. You can acknowledge to yourself how you feel and what you believe. It's the voice in your head that must change. It's up to you to claim your right to your voice and to stand tall in the face of others' judgments. If you believe in yourself, you'll always be at peace. You'll finally silence the hurtful judgments in your head—those most often spoken in the dark of night.

If you want to be a step closer to finding your purpose, you must acknowledge and feel your anger. Any cause that's close to your heart requires an awareness that things can't stay the same, and that change is long overdue. Your motivation will come from your desire to make things better. To speak up, stand up, donate money, or offer your time and services, you must understand that this can only effectively happen when you're angry at the present state of things. Anger is powerful when it's directed toward positive change.

Anger has to travel somewhere. It's either acted on or acted out. When you feel entitled to your feelings, you'll find your voice. It's self-doubt that keeps you silent even in the confines of your mind.

When I began writing this book, I was fueled by my anger toward all of us playing down who we are to appease another. Having to accommodate, acquiesce, profess to, and shapeshift ourselves into what others need so we feel we belong somewhere is a disgrace.

I become furious when I think of the beautiful, innocent children we once were hiding and stuffing our true expressions just to survive the dysfunction of childhood. We escape, but not unscathed for we grow up believing we're unworthy and not good enough. There isn't a client I coach that doesn't share the *not good enough* story with me. I'm exhausted for all of us; this has to stop.

The great news is that correction is possible. Once we stop People-Pleasing, we regain our expression, wonder, curiosity, and fascination for life and people because we're no longer invested in or feel threatened by others' judgments or lack of approval. The focus shifts toward ourselves and our newfound love interest.

Make a list of the things that make you angry. I'm certain you'll find that your purpose and calling lie somewhere on that list. If you're willing to connect to these issues to discover the direct knowledge, experience, and skills in what brings a rise in you, then you'll likely find your purpose quickly.

I remember meeting a woman, Shirley, some years ago who asked me if I'd like to speak to forty-five women that very night. She worked for a makeup company that sold product by hosting parties, which were also used to recruit new salespeople.

I thought to myself, *Off the cuff? I don't have time to prepare.*

"Sure," I said. I closed my eyes, and People-Pleasing came to mind. On some level, I knew that it was negatively impacting my life, and I was angry about it. I found a calling.

Not only did I speak with passion to Shirley's group that night, but I also had the opportunity to say *no* in front of the group, which gave me the perfect segue into my presentation.

Everyone sat at a long, L-shaped table. Before each person was a bowl of water, some cleansing products, and a towel. Shirley asked if she could do a skin treatment on me before my speech. It would require me to wash my face.

"No," I said. "I don't feel comfortable giving a speech with no makeup on my face and with cream all over it." I shared this exchange with the group when I spoke.

"In the past," I told them, "I would have accommodated Shirley and stood up here embarrassed about not looking put together. This experience is the perfect example of what a People Pleaser does: compromising and violating herself to please another."

The group nodded in agreement. It appeared that each was thinking about a time in her life when she'd stepped over herself and her comfort to accommodate another. My timely example hit home.

It's also important to note that a purpose and a calling doesn't necessarily mean a vocation or that you'll be blessed with earning a living through what you love doing. Many people work at jobs that have nothing to do with their purpose but still live out their desires in other ways. What's important is that you become creative and use your unique talents and gifts in some area of your life and often enough to feel fulfilled and happy.

What's most important is that you stop living the life you think you should by avoiding being the things you believe you shouldn't be. Living this way is unfulfilling and downright miserable.

Your expression is essential to living *Your Happy Life Realized*. It's more important than who will like you or who won't. If you like you, it won't matter. That's a purpose and calling to be proud of!

CHAPTER 25

THE FORMULA FOR CREATING AN EXTRAORDINARY LIFE

Living well is the best revenge.

~ George Herbert

"How do you stay so happy?" my client, Rachel, asked. "I mean, you've had your struggles. What do you do to stay happy?"

I smiled and answered, "I kick and scream for a bit, and then I look at the bigger picture, which always brings me faith that my life is exactly where it needs to be. I'm grateful for all that I have."

I shared my secret formula for living an extraordinary life and assured her that she could create the life she wants using this formula, too.

"It will help you to navigate the ebbs and flows of life," I said. "Everything depends on the way you see things and how you choose to live as a result."

I consider myself to be a generally content woman. Having the honor and privilege to support people in their lives and relationships is very rewarding. I receive a great deal of love and joy by watching others evolve and create more love in their lives.

For my personal growth, and to make sure I walk my talk to teach accordingly, I look for a perspective that makes sense and brings me joy. There's a difference between putting a positive spin on things versus seeing a greater meaning for all that has happened based on the lessons in my life.

Sometimes, I even find myself being silly and playful, two qualities that weren't present in my childhood and whose absence I believe I resented for years. Having to be invisible and quiet in my home made me miss out on the normal expression children have. Even so, I relish the gifts that came as a result of shutting down.

Being a People Pleaser required I put my own needs and desires aside, although this didn't stop me from dreaming and fantasizing about my life. I had a vibrant imagination. But holding myself back stayed with me into adulthood. Even when I was free to make my own choices and live out my dreams, I held myself in check. On an unconscious level, I believed I wasn't allowed my expression. My dreaming and fantasizing continued, but those dreams and fantasies remained unrealized because of the behavioral pattern of suppressing my expression that began in my childhood. People-Pleasing as an adult made sure I stayed invisible and unfulfilled.

We're all searching for autonomy. Wearing the People Pleaser persona cuts off our ability for self-expression. We want to express ourselves, but our behavior won't allow it. We're at a loss, and we're not even aware of it. To compensate, many People Pleasers become stubborn, inflexible, impatient, intolerable, and frustrated. Even though their oppositional behavior doesn't feel good to them, it's what these People Pleasers know as their individual expression. But they don't have to stay in opposition, and neither do you. The key is transforming the whole of you—how you think, act, and present in the world. As you move further into the process, you'll be amazed at how your life changes, sometimes almost effortlessly. When you find this happening, you're experiencing the Law of Attraction.

I was skeptical when I first learned about the Law of Attraction and how we can powerfully call into our lives the things we desire. Despite my skepticism, I was at a low point in my life, so I was open to learning new things. Depression can be very motivating at times.

I became intrigued the more I studied and learned about this law that connects everything by energy, frequencies, and vibrations.

I began analyzing myself more deeply to uncover what I was thinking and feeling.

If you'd like to learn more about the Law of Attraction, you'll find a wealth of information online. Also, when you visit my website to collect your gift, you'll gain access to some of my preferred choices on this subject. Visit www.LessonsLearnedInLove.com.

Years ago, I attended a powerful workshop about manifestation and how we can attract positive experiences in our lives by what we think, feel, and say. As I listened intently to the speaker, I had a sudden, unexpected epiphany that sent me into tears. At that moment, I realized my ongoing sadness stemmed from not allowing myself to live out my desires. I was withholding from myself, and this created a misalignment with my soul.

"If you're not living out your desires, you'll get sick," the speaker explained.

I had become a master of disguise, convincing myself that what I needed and wanted was insignificant. I'd completely forgotten what I was interested in or made me happy. I was still confused even after having this epiphany. More time needed to pass before I could connect many of the dots in my life. I dedicated myself to dig deep, and I believe I've found the most effective steps to create an extraordinary life. Keep in mind that following these steps is an ongoing process. What I've found is that they're working magically for me. I believe that you will also have great success with these steps if you're willing to commit the time and effort necessary to make their lessons stick.

As you read the formula below, keep in mind that each step requires perspective and action on your part. I encourage and invite you to do the exercises in previous chapters that support People Pleaser reform before following this formula. These steps will make more sense if you do, and you'll be in a better position to follow along.

Formula for an Extraordinary Life

Complete the six steps in order.

Feel, Feel, Feel

+ *Kick and Scream*

+ *Ask Questions*

+ *Consider the Bigger Picture*

+ *Ask to be shown what you can't see*

+ *Receive direction and guidance*

= *An Extraordinary Life*

1. **Feel, Feel, Feel.** It's time to be with all of your feelings even the darkest ones you don't want to have. Feelings, when allowed and not resisted, will move through you and dissolve. Have you ever experienced a profound sadness such as grief where you couldn't hold back your feelings and cried uncontrollably? That's an example of how the release of feelings cleanses you of the sad energy.

2. **Kick and Scream.** Take time by yourself to physically move the energy of your feelings. Beat a pillow, lock yourself in your car and

scream, hit a punching bag, dance to hard rock music. It's a crucial time to give your feelings movement and purpose. Complain and vent to trusted friends who are willing to listen. Stop avoiding being negative. We all need to be negative at times. It's realistic. If you resist and hold back your negative feelings, they'll fester, and you'll just be pretending you feel good when you don't. All your anger, annoyance, frustration, and angst can be released by acting on your feelings with movement both vocal and physical.

3. **Ask Questions.** Powerful questions will open you up to allowing answers that support insights and epiphanies. My late teacher and mentor, Debbie Ford, was a master at creating powerful questions that provided profound answers. I recommend her book, *The Right Questions*. Carry it with you wherever you go. Examples of simple, powerful questions:

   - Why is this challenge in my life right now, and what lesson can I gain from my experience with it?

   - Why did this person come into my life, and what do they have to teach me?

   - What do I know now that I wouldn't have known had I not lived through this situation?

4. **Consider the Bigger Picture.** With the answers you've received to the questions you asked yourself in step three, and considering that everything happens for a reason, speculate on your journey and see the "big picture." Connect to how all your experiences supported you in arriving here at this time in your life and how your present experiences are taking you to higher ground. The "big picture" is the purpose of your life. Focus on the importance of each experience.

5. **Ask to be Shown What You Can't See**. If you're not getting answers to questions and having difficulty seeing the big picture, ask God, the Universe, the Angels or whatever higher power you believe in to support you in obtaining answers and clarity. When I have a hard time getting answers, I ask God to guide me to see what it is I'm not seeing. Ask, and you shall receive! I *always* get answers.

6. **Receive Direction and Guidance.** This crucial step requires you have trust and faith that you're being guided to an outcome that will serve you. If it looks different than the outcome you desire, you must shift your direction and trust that you don't always know what's best.

   A friend of mine has reinvented her business several times to no avail. She's been given other opportunities along the way and missed them because she's invested in and adamant about this business. She can't see that everything has been pointing her toward something else. She struggles tremendously, which is whittling away at her self-confidence and ability to see things any differently.

When things are aligned, and you're being directed toward a certain outcome, resources will show up, people will come into your life, and it will seem as if things are working out. When things are misaligned or opposed, this is a red flag. When things are hard, it's crucial that you open up to allow yourself to see other opportunities. It doesn't mean giving up on your present circumstance; it means opening up to see other options. Once you do this, you'll know if there's another fork in the road that's a better direction to take.

Personal Tip: If I'm conflicted when making a specific choice after I've followed all these necessary steps, I close my eyes and imagine each scenario. In between, I breathe, open my eyes, breathe again, and close my eyes, making sure each scenario has its own time and space in my awareness. Whichever scenario feels the best in my physical body, is the one I choose. So far, it's worked like a charm.

I believe that what we consider the mistakes and regrets in our lives are what we see in hindsight. It's important to recognize whether you knew something was a bad choice at the time you chose it. That's what I call a mistake. It's important to learn, heed the lesson, and move on.

For choices we see as wrong in hindsight, it pays to remember they were the right choices *at the time*. If they brought about unfavorable results it's because: there was a lesson that needed to be learned, you may have ignored something along the way, you were attached to a particular outcome and didn't take the direction being offered, or you simply sabotaged yourself. It's all a good learning process.

My greatest recommendation for living an extraordinary life is to *always* be true to you. Always choose yourself first and vow never to allow yourself to be knowingly and voluntarily compromised or violated another minute of another day. Cherish the gift God has given you. Always do your due diligence and get to know who you are so that you can stop People-Pleasing and start serving the world! Now that's a worthy pursuit!

CHAPTER 26

WHAT'S NEXT?

No one can go back and make a brand-new start.
Anyone can start from now and make
a brand-new ending.

~ Carl Bard

When I think of how much time I have left on this planet, I know that even if I live to a ripe old age, I've already lived over half of my life. I intend to live my life happily, peacefully, and intimately connected to myself and others. I find my greatest joy lies in the meaning I give to everything. That's pretty much the bottom line.

No matter where you are in your life, there's always the opportunity for correction and the choice to create an extraordinary life. It takes willingness, commitment, and most of all, desire. It's up to you. No one will do this for you.

I'm a firm believer that People-Pleasing behavior is the number one problem in many people's lives because it interferes with correction and growth and it kills desire. It's like kryptonite to Superman. It weakens you and eats away at your strength and power.

I also believe that fear gets a bad rap. Fear is one of our greatest motivators. Fear can push us into action as nothing else can. I strongly suggest and encourage you to listen closely to your fear because it has vital information for you.

By the time my clients reach me, they're pretty much at the end of their rope. They're certain they can't take any added pain or drama. Once they commit to coaching, they experience radical growth. Fear becomes the motivator.

So, if you're scared about embarking on the People-Pleasing reform path, I empathize with you and invite you to feel the fear and move forward anyway. Know that you're losing as long as you keep People-Pleasing. It's time to start winning.

If you've read through to this point, but haven't yet done the exercises, I highly encourage you to review them and begin. If you've done the exercises, are starting to feel the shifts of People Pleaser reform, and want to delve deeper, visit my site PeoplePleasersReformAcademy.com (for women) and SayNoToYesDear.com (for men). Once you join, you'll receive more information from me as well as an invitation to join my private Facebook page.

You're welcome to join both sites to read or participate in the conversation. I think it's helpful to recognize the People-Pleasing expression in all of us. Both sites will also lead you to my coaching site, LessonsLearnedInLove.com, where you can learn more about private coaching and request a free consultation if you feel inclined to do so.

Wherever you are right now, I invite you to add the following daily practices to your life so that you're in the best position to bring about the experiences you desire.

Set Intentions

An intention is a declaration to yourself and the Universe of what you would like to experience. When I wake up each morning, I set an intention for the day such as, *"I set the intention for this day to be peaceful, inspiring, and full of insights."* When I ask myself at the end of the day if my intention was met, I always find strong indicators to prove positive. I also find it helpful to set several intentions throughout the day as I end one activity and begin a new one. *"I set the intention to move forward from this person, persons, or activity and to leave all energies behind to evaporate into the air. I choose not to carry any conversations discussed or any negativity that transpired into my day. I also ask that others be free of my energy as well. And as I embark on this new activity, I ask that it be pleasurable, fun, and memorable."* I'm amazed at how setting intentions support the outcome I'm looking to experience. I also notice that when things don't go smoothly, it's either because it's time for a challenge and lesson, or

I simply forgot to set an intention. Living deliberately and consciously is important. You have more control than you think.

Clear Energies

Everything in the Universe, including you, is made up of energy. If you find yourself feeling exhausted all the time or lack the energy to do what you need to in the day, it's very likely because you're carrying a lot of negative energy with you. Too much of it can suck the life out of you.

I like to imagine myself in a bubble of light that helps to protect me from other people's negative or excitable energies and protect them from mine as well. We all carry both positive and negative energies, and it's not healthy to take in too much of either. We can't prevent exchanging energy with each other, but we can have some control over how much gets in or out if we consciously choose to use tools. The bubble of light works well, as you can feel separated and safe with this imaginary protective shield. It will support you in knowing that you're taking measures to address your self-care and respect others, too.

Another way I clear energy is to say something after each encounter with people that helps my energy stay strong and positive. You can use mine or create something personal for yourself: *"Please clear all negative energies exchanged in the experience I just had with (fill in name) or all the people in the supermarket, the bank, etc., and keep my energy at a strong, high vibration as I move on through my day."* As I say this, I use my hands to imagine that I'm washing the old energy off my body to be absorbed into the ground below. The force I'm addressing is God, the Archangels, or the Universe. Whatever you believe in will suffice.

Send Loving Energy to Yourself and Others

The most loving thing you can do for yourself and others is to use your imagination and see the best-case scenario for anything or anyone you're concerned or worried about. It doesn't help to dwell in the negative or in what can go wrong. I caution you to be aware that too much negative thinking can bring about negative experiences that can spiral into more negative thinking as a result. It's our choice as to how we want to see things. Your mind-set and emotional state have more impact than you know.

Count Your Blessings

At the end of each day and throughout the day, step into the knowledge that you're blessed. Don't be distracted by the busyness of your life and lose out on what matters: the people and animals you love, the roof over your head, the food you enjoy, and so on. I keep a gratitude jar on my night table and make sure to write down what I'm grateful for every day.

Keep a Journal

Write down your feelings. While you're reforming from People-Pleasing, a lot of things will come up. If you're not getting outside support, a journal is the next best thing. Keep a record, and revisit and read it often to learn more about your feelings and how you see yourself, others, and the world. You'll begin to discover insights and epiphanies, especially when you start to notice patterns or the same challenges happening repeatedly. You can't change anything you don't acknowledge, and you can't acknowledge anything you're unaware of. A journal is a great awareness tool.

Stay Clear of What Brings You Down

Become super-focused on the people, places, and things that bring you down and stay clear. If it's someone you can't avoid, such as a coworker or family member, set strong intentions and keep yourself in a positive mind-set. Keep your distance as much as you can. Surround yourself with things that inspire you. Keep a list of powerful mantras close by and say them silently to yourself when you're in the presence of people or things that bring you down. Remember, you always have control over how you feel. Don't give them power and don't take the bait.

Learn from Others

Don't forget that you're gifted with teachers in your life. Some will bring positive experiences and others will bring challenges.

Those who are challenging bring the more important lessons for you to learn. Pay close attention. The people you judge the most have much to teach you.

Teach Others

At all costs, never reward bad behavior. It will disempower you and everyone else. Even though we want to minimize our reactive behavior, you must understand that you aren't perfect and that you're a teacher for others, too. Your reactive behavior is just an explosion or implosion of feelings and expression resistance, so it comes out uncensored. At these times, forgive yourself and recognize the opportunity to grow for someone else who may have needed your harsh reaction. It's not about going around biting off heads but understanding that sometimes you can't hold things back. There's value in drama, too.

Acknowledge Yourself Daily

If we added up the minutes, hours, days, weeks, and years we've spent beating ourselves up for one thing or another, we'll hardly even out the score if we're to give ourselves our thanks for everything we do on our behalf every second of every day. The scales will still tip in favor of the negative. Either way, acknowledging ourselves many times during the day will support us in turning our lives around and moving toward the love we all yearn for. I can't stress enough how viewing yourself as your primary support, your greatest ally, your loyal confidant, and your sacred self will bring about the love and joy you've always wanted. It will also position you in the best place to attract healthy love from others.

I'm rooting for you and feel certain that as you reform from the destructive behavior that has misled you, you'll find your way back to your arms which have been waiting to embrace you for far too long.

I intend to continue sharing with you on my sites and in books to come. Until then, I wish you *Your Happy Life Realized*. You deserve it, and the world deserves you!

Warmly, Eve

EPILOGUE

As with any experience in life, writing this book had within it a journey all its own. Along with the cathartic personal expression it offered—the honor and privilege to share insights, epiphanies, and recommended practices with you and the joy of accomplishing an important goal—I couldn't have expected the greater gift that awaited me.

When my editor, Lis, sent me an email close to the deadline for returning the manuscript to me, I was surprised that her critique wasn't more favorable. In the most tender words Lis could muster, she let me know her honest opinion, for which I'm forever grateful. Even though she enjoyed my content, stories, and mission to warn others of the dangers of People-Pleasing, she felt the order of the chapters could be improved, and she offered to revise it. But to do so would mean many more months would pass before the book could be published.

As I listened carefully with an open heart and mind on our phone conversation that followed, I realized that my impression was more important than any critique being offered, even though I'm a believer in listening to feedback and owning it. I knew I could have rewritten the book five times in an attempt to make it perfect. But I already felt that the manuscript was good and strong. It needed to get into the hands of People Pleasers who are struggling *now*. I was prepared for some people to like it and others to not. So, if you take anything away from this book, I hope the message that *what you think is what counts most* gets through. I walk my talk.

I said, *"No"* graciously and received the complete edited manuscript back a few days later.

I read the first forty pages upon the manuscript's arrival. I was disappointed that I didn't enjoy reading it. I wondered what happened to the original excitement, joy, and pride I had felt when I sent it off for editing. I contemplated her offer of taking several more months to work on the book.

I then reread those same pages in the wee hours of the morning when I couldn't sleep due to the anxiety that had arisen from hearing a reputable professional say my manuscript *could be more powerful.* I read slowly to capture every word. By page ten, I was lit up like a Christmas tree! Not only did I thoroughly enjoy what I was reading, I felt, once again, proud of my book and overjoyed that it would soon be available to people who wanted support in their lives and relationships.

My experience with Lis birthed a greater gift than just a stupendously edited manuscript. As I processed what was clouding my impression of my writing, I discovered that even though I consciously liked what I'd created, when someone else responded less favorably, their impression is what I retained in my unconscious. This experience revealed a long, ingrained pattern that still remained in the driver's seat of my life telling me *I wasn't good enough.*

Even though I told Lis that I liked how I constructed the flow of my book and was proud of it, my unconscious psyche took over once I began reading. I was looking for what was wrong while skimming the words in front of me, wondering what it was she didn't like. I made an *unconscious decision* not to like it either. I fell back into making the automatic assumption that she was right and her opinion about my book was more important than mine.

If that isn't a huge People-Pleasing trait that has us hide under a rock and disappear, I don't know what is!

And just like that, as quickly as the wind was taken out of my sails, I was up again heading for a bright horizon.

By writing and reading this book, I, too, learned more ways to recognize my People-Pleasing ways and what I still need to be aware of as I continue the process of reforming.

I began dancing like no one was watching, and I haven't stopped since.

Notes

Chapter 7:

1. "What is an Addiction?" *Psychology Today*, https://www.psychologytoday.com/us/basics/addiction.

Chapter 9:

1. Ali McGraw and Ryan O'Neal. *Love Story*. Directed by Arthur Hiller. Los Angeles, CA: Paramount Pictures, 1970.
2. "Personal Boundaries," Wikipedia, May 29, 2018, https://en.wikipedia.org/wiki/personal_boundaries.

Chapter 12:

1. "Codependency," Wikipedia, August 30, 2018, https://en.wikipedia.org/wiki/codependency.

Chapter 16:

1. Bruno Mars, vocalist, "When I was Your Man," by Bruno Mars, Philip Lawrence, Ari Levine, and Andrew Wyatt, December 7, 2012, track 6 on Unorthodox Jukebox, Atlantic Records.

Chapter 19:

1. "Loser." Merriam-Webster, Accessed July 2018, https://www.merriam-webster.com/dictionary/loser.
2. "Liar." Merriam-Webster, Accessed July 2018, https://www.merriam-webster.com/dictionary/liar.
3. "Phony." Merriam-Webster, Accessed July 2018, https://www.merriam-webster.com/dictionary/phony.
4. "Fraud." Merriam-Webster, Accessed July 2018, https://www.merriam-webster.com/dictionary/fraud.

ADDITIONAL RESOURCES

You can never have too many resources. Here are three that I highly recommend.

1. David Hawkins, *Dealing with the CrazyMakers in Your Life: Setting Boundaries on Unhealthy Relationships*, Eugene, OR, Harvest House Publishers, 2007.

2. Phil McGraw, *Life Code: The New Rules for Winning in the Real World*, Los Angeles, CA, Bird Street Books, Inc., 2012.

3. Margaret Paul and Erika Chopich, *Healing Your Aloneness: Finding Love and Wholeness Through Your Inner Child*, New York, NY, Harper Collins, 1990.

ABOUT THE AUTHOR

Eve Rosenberg is an Integrative Life Coach who compassionately supports others to step into their lives with both feet and create relationships that are joyful and intimate with themselves and others.

Born to Holocaust survivors and hoping to save their unhappy marriage, Eve has experienced trauma and drama in her life. As an avid People Pleaser for decades, she understands how this destructive behavior has wreaked havoc in her relationships. Chasing love through the opinions and accolades of others, she knows what it's like to feel lonely, unworthy, and lost. She also knows with certainty that despite what we have lived through, there's correction and renewal available whenever we're ready to claim it.

"Everything that has taken me to today has been for a reason; therefore, I love yesterday, embrace today, and cherish tomorrow."

Along with being trained as a Master Integrative Coach by the late Debbie Ford and the Ford Institute for Transformational Training, Eve holds a Bachelor of Arts degree in Sociology/Psychology and certification as a Holistic Health and Wellness Counselor. She also has a vast employment history in corporate America. Eve lives in sunny Florida with her two dogs, Tabitha and Priscilla.

Made in the USA
Columbia, SC
19 December 2018